Copyright © 2008 by Steven Rosenfeld

978-0-9752724-5-9

All rights reserved. No part of this book may be reproduced in any form, except brief excerpts for the purpose of review, without written permission of the publisher.

ALTERNET BOOKS
77 Federal Street, 2nd Floor
San Francisco, CA 94107
www.alternet.org
books@alternet.org

Cover by Jess Morphew
Interior by Daniel Ridge

LIBRARY OF CONGRESS CATALOGING-IN-PUBLICATION DATA

Rosenfeld, Steven, 1959-
  Count my vote : a citizen's guide to voting / by Steven Rosenfeld. -- 1st ed.
    p. cm.
  ISBN 978-0-9752724-5-9
  1. Voting--United States. 2. Voter registration--United States. 3. Presidents--United States--Election--2008. 4. Elections--United State. I. Title.

JK1976.R66 2008
324.60973--dc22
                            2008022205

First printing, 2008

1 2 3 4 5 6 7 8 9 10 – 12 11 10 09 08

This book is printed with soy-based ink by a union Canadian printer using 100% post-consumer fiber, which is processed chlorine free, Forest Stewardship Council (FSC) certified, and manufactured using biogas energy.

Steven Rosenfeld

To all who cherish their right to vote.

Contents

Foreword by Don Hazen   1

PART ONE

Introduction   3

Chapter One
Voter Registration   17

Chapter Two
Student Voting   33

Chapter Three
Absentee Voting   39

Chapter Four
Voting Machines and Election Officials   47

Chapter Five
Election Day Reminders/Getting Involved   59

PART TWO
State-by-State Voting Guide   63

Nationwide Voting Resource List   115
Notes   118
Acknowledgments   122
About the Author   123
AlterNet Citizen Publishers   124
About AlterNet   128
About AlterNet Books   129

Foreword

It's clear that 2008 is a watershed year for progressives. We've got that mix of momentum and hope. Record turnout in this year's presidential primary contests bodes well for the change our country needs this fall when we go to the polls. But we can't leave it to chance. We need to make sure every vote counts.

That's what this book is about. We know bad things can happen on Election Day. Remember Florida in 2000 and Ohio in 2004? The failures in our "democratic" system made me furious. They made millions of us angry. And frankly, we felt impotent, too.

So AlterNet decided to do something about it. We were determined to do our part to ensure history would not repeat itself by standing up for the most fundamental right in a democracy: the right to vote.

For a year, our reporter, Steven Rosenfeld, has been covering elections from a voting rights perspective. He has looked at the barriers to voting and the victories for voters. Before joining AlterNet, he co-wrote and edited two books on what went wrong in the 2004 presidential election. Before the election, there was no book that warned voters of possible problems and gave them the tools and the knowledge to surmount obstacles.

Foreword

The dirty secret is that some candidates do better when less people vote, so their strategy is to make it as hard as possible in order to discourage people. That's called voter suppression. We were determined to prevent that from happening in a history-making year. We want everyone who is eligible to vote. This is America after all.

We've taken what Steven has learned from his reporting, looked at the track record and lessons from 2008's presidential primaries, consulted with voter registration groups and voter advocates and then turned all that information into an indispensable voter handbook.

Count My Vote is for everyone who will be registering voters or working on campaigns or who wants to vote and has questions. The book is filled with what people need to know about each state's voting rules, voter ID laws, new voting machines, what to do if you move, and what to do if problems crop up. It has special sections for students, seniors, and a state-by-state voting reference guide. But most importantly, it helps voters have confidence that they can handle any problems they face while voting.

We also asked AlterNet readers to support this effort, and over 1,300 of them responded with contributions as Citizen Publishers. Thank you, donors, for your history-making support, which will help get books to non-profit organizations that intend to register 750,000 new voters by the fall.

Count My Vote is our effort to keep the spotlight on any attempts to twist the rules and discourage voters. Included are the basic tools for fair voting—a bedrock from which we can change our country for the better. The book provides the kind of solutions that progressives can be proud of—a handbook for citizens who want to make a difference in our democracy.

—*Don Hazen, June 2008*

Introduction

AMERICANS BELIEVE IN VOTING. Even if we do not all like the results, Americans of all political persuasions deeply believe in voting—and the power of elections to steer society and chart the future. It is a common tie that binds our diverse and divergent lives.

Voting is many things. It is a hope. It is a responsibility. It is exciting. And occasionally, voting in the United States is not always easy or without difficulties. Depending on your age or race, this may be obvious or may come as a surprise. But even in the early 21st century, a host of things can complicate or even prevent the act of casting a vote in an election.

You might not be properly registered or have the required form of identification; you may not know the location of your polling place, or you may be daunted by long lines and a shortage of voting machines. Poll workers may tell you your name does not appear on voter lists, that you already voted, or that you were supposed to vote by mail. You might be unfamiliar with new voting technology or make a mistake while voting.

These were the most common problems documented during 2008's presidential primaries. More than half of the complaints made to the 1-866-MYVOTE1 hotline during the first 10 primaries of 2008 were from callers who were not properly registered or didn't know the location of

Introduction

their polling places.[1] But in most cases, people endured these setbacks and succeeded at voting anyway, leading to many of the highest turnouts in primaries in years.

A number of obstacles may confront voters in the upcoming election. Our goal is to help people clear these hurdles, should they arise. It is our hope that anyone with a real interest in elections, from campaign workers to seasoned ballot-casters to first-time voters, will note the possible pitfalls and take steps to avoid them, so more Americans will be able to exercise their right to vote. In American elections, it's the fine print of the process that can discourage people from voting. Voters need to make sure their registration is valid, know the location of their polling place, present the form of identification required by their state, tolerate long lines or delays, and be ready to speak up if their right to vote is challenged for any reason.

> **"Americans of all political persuasions deeply believe in voting. But voting in the United States is not always easy or without difficulties."**

The first half of this handbook examines the starting place of the voting process—voter registration. We pay special attention to groups that have historically experienced barriers to voting: new voters, students, low-income people, people of color, seniors, and overseas voters, including members of the military. You'll also find sections on voting by mail, basics about new voting machines and interacting with poll workers, what to do if problems arise on Election Day, and suggestions on how to get more involved. In the second half of the book we summarize key points for each of the 50 states, including registration rules and filing deadlines, election officials to contact, voter ID requirements, voting machines, potential problems to look out for based on the 2008 primaries, and early voting options.

Introduction

The rest of the introduction illuminates the major voting trends of 2008. The results of recent presidential and some congressional elections have left many Americans wary of the electoral process. It's our hope that informing and educating the public about voting will help bring about elections that everyone can trust—no matter who wins.

EXPECT RECORD TURNOUT

ONE TREND WE CAN BE SURE OF is that turnout for November's election is going to be *huge*. In 2004, 122 million people voted; that's 61 percent of registered voters, the highest turnout since 1968.[2] The figure is likely to be even higher in November, given that voters came out in unprecedented numbers during the primary season. On Super Tuesday, February 5, voter participation records were set in 15 states, with 12 states setting records for Democrats and 11 states setting records for Republicans.[3] As the contest between Democrats Barack Obama and Hillary Clinton continued into the spring, late-voting states also saw sizeable jumps in new voter registrations.[4]

The effect of record turnout will vary among states and counties, but at the very least it means people can expect lines in some places as poll workers check in voters. However, many other things can also cause delays and these often are not the fault of voters. During 2008's primaries, for example, counties in several states, including California, Maryland, and Indiana, ran out of paper ballots.

Several other factors could stop people from getting inside the voting booth as well.

Introduction

SCRAMBLED DATABASES

SOME STATES WILL BE USING a new statewide database of voters for the first time in a presidential election. The idea behind these databases, which are required under a 2002 federal law, was to shift the management of elections from local officials to the state, so elections could be administered more uniformly. Unfortunately, the solution to old problems generated some new ones.

Even before the first primary of 2008, journalists were reporting that new statewide voter lists were erroneously removing eligible voters. In early January, database malfunctions were dubbed the "sleeper issue of 2008," after New Jersey, Maine, Oregon, Montana, and Alaska mistakenly deleted the names of some people who voted in 2006.[5] In primaries this year in New Mexico, Arizona, and California, individuals waited for hours to vote "only to find they weren't listed as registered voters—or they weren't listed in the party of their choice," the Associated Press reported in March.[6] There were similar reports from Maryland,[7] the District of Columbia,[8] Pennsylvania,[9] and North Carolina,[10] based on news reports and calls to voter hotlines.

One recurring database problem was caused when a voter's name was missing or misspelled and did not match other state lists, such as driver's licenses or emergency 911 system addresses, which were used to verify voter registrations. In early 2008 in Florida, election officials wanted to remove 14,000 such names. Florida law blocks registering people whose names or identification numbers cannot be verified in the state's driver's license or Social Security database. The Florida State Conference of the NAACP sued the state, saying those people were disproportionately Hispanic and African-American voters who had been denied the right to register to vote since 2006 because their names were misspelled in other state records, or due to typos in entering their data. In December 2007, a

Introduction

federal judge decided in favor of the voters and the state was forced to add 14,000 Floridians to the voter rolls. In April 2008 a federal appeals court reversed that decision.[11]

Also in Florida, another federal court ruled in March 2008 that all registration information has to be submitted accurately at least 29 days before an election, with no grace period for making corrections.[12] In other words, the responsibility for getting it right rests with the voter, not the government. Voters whose names have changed as a result of marriage, divorce, or other reasons; whose names are hyphenated; or who have recently moved cannot assume the new statewide voter lists have correctly included them. The solution, no matter where you live, is to contact your local election office and verify your voter registration.

> "Voters whose names have changed or who have recently moved cannot assume the new statewide voter lists have correctly included them. The solution, no matter where you live, is to contact your local election office and verify your voter registration."

VOTER ID

RESTRICTIVE STATE VOTER IDENTIFICATION LAWS present another potential snag. All states require voters to present some form of identification before voting. The most rigorous require a government-issue photo ID, such as a passport or driver's license. While most adults have such IDs, many others, such as students, seniors, and low-income people, do not. One 2007 study found that 13 percent of legal voters lacked government-issue photo identification.[13]

In April, the Supreme Court upheld Indiana's toughest-in-the-nation voter ID law, which requires a government-issue photo ID. The ruling

Introduction

prompted a handful of other states to consider passing similar laws. By mid-May, legislators in Missouri had hoped to adopt a stricter voter ID law to take effect by November.[14] The law would have required voters to present a government photo ID before voting and proof of citizenship in order to register to vote. Critics said the legislation could cause more than 200,000 people to lose their right to vote.[15] After public protests, the proposal died when it was not taken up before Missouri's Legislature adjourned.

This is a fierce political fight, and the outcome will affect a lot of people. Supporters say that rigorous voter-identification laws deter imposters from casting fraudulent votes. Critics maintain the regulations discourage potential voters who lack the time or the means to obtain the required forms of ID. For the elderly and the poor especially, acquiring birth certificates or other official documents can be costly, time consuming and difficult to navigate the bureaucracy. After the November 2007 election, it was not hard to find such cases in Indiana,[16] as well as Georgia and Michigan.[17]

The Lawyers' Committee for Civil Rights Under Law reported that during Indiana's May 6 primary, elderly people (including nuns in their 80s and 90s), students attempting to use school ID cards, and an American serviceman attempting to use his military ID were all prevented from voting because they lacked the required photo IDs.[18] In Arizona, the first and only state so far to require documented proof of citizenship when registering to vote, about 38,000, or 17 percent, of applications have been rejected since 2004 when the law took effect, according to Michael Slater of Project Vote.[19] This potential barrier targets a wider segment of society than just minorities—Slater says that half of married women lack birth certificates with their married names. Elderly and poor people often do not have their birth certificates, as well.[20]

Voters should find out in advance what type of ID their state requires and bring it with them on Election Day. A healthy supply of patience may

Introduction

also come in handy, since voter hotlines during the primaries reported that some poll workers were unsure which IDs were acceptable and asked voters to wait while they checked.[21] All states have voter ID laws, but Florida, Georgia, Hawaii, Indiana, Louisiana, Michigan, and South Dakota require government photo IDs.[22]

While the Supreme Court's Indiana decision gives momentum to states like Missouri and Texas that have been debating voter ID issues for years,[23] only a few states could adopt new photo ID laws before November,[24] since their 2008 legislative sessions are over or almost over. As of June 1, states with active photo ID requirement bills were Illinois, Mississippi, North Carolina, New Jersey, Pennsylvania, and Rhode Island, according to Project Vote. In contrast, states with active bills requiring proof of citizenship when registering to vote were California, Illinois, and Michigan.[25]

The biggest ID-related concerns awaiting voters this fall are likely to be confusion among poll workers, potential discrimination, and implementation of new laws, said Tova A. Wang of the nonpartisan election reform group Common Cause.[26] In later chapters we'll discuss how voters can deal with these issues.

NEW VOTING TECHNOLOGY

MOST STATES ARE USING different types of voting machines than in the past two presidential elections. A handful of states will be using different equipment than in 2006. The vast majority of votes will be cast using two basic types of voting systems. With the first system, direct-recording electronic (DRE) voting, voters touch a computer screen, punch buttons, or turn dials to vote, and the votes are recorded directly into computer memory. The second system uses a paper ballot that is marked by a voter's pen but counted by a computer scanner. (New York and Idaho are still using older, mechanical-lever voting machines and computer punch cards, respectively.)

DRE voting has caused widespread controversy. A growing number of election activists, scientists, and some secretaries of state have criticized these systems because they rely entirely on the correctness of the underlying software and provide no independent means of verification. In contrast, paper ballots can be hand-counted in close contests and recounts. In response to critics, many states that use DREs now require them to produce a paper record the voter can verify before casting an electronic vote. While the "voter-verified paper trail," or VVPAT, printers do not solve the software issues posed by DREs, voters still should take the time to see if their vote is being correctly noted.

There are also practical problems with DREs. Despite training, election officials do not always know how to use the newest voting machines, leading to delayed opening of polls in several states.[27] Some states are returning to systems using paper ballots and computer scanners. Florida and most of California made this transition by mid-2008. Some counties in Ohio, Iowa, and

> **If there's a voting machine problem, voters should stop and ask poll workers for help or ask to use another machine. If their county uses a paper trail printer, they should check to see if their vote is being properly recorded.**

Colorado also switched, although it is difficult to predict which machinery they will use in November. Individual counties in Pennsylvania have also moved in this direction.

While DRE technology has been criticized, it is undeniably part of the landscape in 2008. More attuned voters can go to county websites and learn how the machines work before voting. If a machine is malfunctioning, voters should stop and ask poll workers for help—including using another

Introduction

machine. If their county uses a VVPAT printer, voters should always check to see if their vote is being properly recorded. If the printout is wrong, they should talk to a poll worker before casting their vote electronically. Should the problem recur, they should ask to use another machine and then call a voter hotline (1-866-OUR-VOTE or 1-866-MYVOTE1) or a nearby presidential campaign office. Either will help contact election officials to have the machine pulled from use.

Some voting rights lawyers also suggest calling the local Board of Elections or agency charged with administering the election to lodge a formal complaint, or the secretary of state or state's chief election officer.[28] If a problem requires court intervention, judges typically will ask lawyers representing voters if they sought a prior solution with the responsible parties. Courts are reluctant to intervene if other remedies have not been tried first.

Tolerance and a civil tone will go a long way toward making sure you are casting your vote properly—especially if you need a poll worker's help with a malfunctioning piece of equipment. In some states and counties, emergency paper ballots will be available as backup should problems arise (although voters may have to remind poll workers of that option).

Another factor that may complicate voting in 2008 is that local governments may not have purchased enough voting machines for a high turnout, causing bottlenecks at the polls. At an April congressional hearing on the primary season's election problems, April Pye, interim director of the Fulton County Board of Elections in Georgia, an Atlanta suburb, said officials in her state all faced budget cuts "due to a very depressed economy."[29] She spoke *after* high turnout in Georgia's primary created hours-long delays for thousands of people because of a shortage of computers to check in voters with a new electronic voting system.

Introduction

Although poll workers generally try to accommodate people while following their state's election laws, voters should still be prepared for delays or snags. Allowing extra time to vote will take the pressure off all involved.

WHOSE CONFUSION AT THE POLLS?

ALL THESE FACTORS, individually or collectively, can cause confusion at the polls. Perhaps the most ironic headline from 2008's primary season came from Tucson, Arizona, where the *Arizona Daily Star* declared, "Election Problems Linked to Turnout"—an indirect way of saying that if voters had just stayed home everything would have been fine.[30] But the article's opening did note the basic trends: "Record turnout, voter confusion, and short-staffed polling places on Tuesday produced an election as notable for long lines and names missing from the voter rolls as for the results."

According to the article, Pima County elections director Brad Nelson blamed voters for "the spike in provisional ballots," which are issued when people are not on voter rolls. The eligibility of voters casting these ballots must be verified after Election Day before they are added to the vote count. Nelson said the high use of provisional ballots was due to "people moving and not updating their voter registrations, or requesting early ballots then not receiving them, or not filling them out." But local activists like John Brakey of AuditAZ, said the county's voter database scrambled thousands of names and listed people as voting by mail when they had not requested an absentee ballot.[31]

Nelson and Brakey are probably both correct. Their explanations do not contradict each other, but illustrate the cascading effect of polling place problems. Voters should be prepared to fight for their right to vote if they see that something is amiss. One early morning voter in North Carolina's May 6 primary discovered that her 18-year-old daughter's name was not

Introduction

in their precinct's poll book. Her persistence revealed that people living on certain streets had not been assigned a precinct, thus they were not listed in poll books. The oversight was cleared up after the woman contacted voting rights activists.[32]

Provisional ballots provide a safety net for voters who might otherwise be denied the opportunity to vote. But about half the states will only count these ballots if they are cast at the precinct where the voter is registered.[33] That means voters have to be in the right polling place; or, if there is a multi-precinct voting center, they must turn in their provisional ballot at their precinct's table. Voters should ask poll workers for their precinct number and double-check when turning in their ballot. In contrast, other states will count provisional ballots cast anywhere in the voter's county.

Staffing is another complicating factor. High-turnout elections mean election administrators need not just more voting machines, but more poll workers. The country has 180,000 polling places, requiring 2 million poll workers. In 2006, the average age for a poll worker was 72.[34]

> "Serving as a poll worker is one of the best ways to protect elections."

Typically, these folks work 14-hour days, are paid $7 an hour, and receive three hours of training.[35] Serving as a poll worker is one of the best ways to protect elections, and assisting with the voting process often means more to these individuals than earning a few extra dollars. Yet as voting becomes increasingly high-tech, poll workers unfamiliar with computers evince a greater potential for frustration.

Poll workers, no matter how well intentioned, can become confused by the minutiae of election law. Here is what one man—an election activist, no less—wrote to colleagues after the Pennsylvania primary: "As an election judge last Tuesday in a heavily minority precinct in Lancaster I can attest to the fact there were several instances of newly registered voters who showed up to vote (in the Democratic primary) but couldn't because they were listed as independent or no party. At no point were we instructed to allow these voters to cast a provisional ballot, and frankly, it did not occur to me to provide them with one."[36] Curiously, the election judge, who runs the precinct, said he did give a provisional ballot to a man who insisted he was a registered Democrat, which is what he should have been doing all along. Voters who know their rights can insist on better treatment.

Many election administrators are acutely aware of the flaws in their voting systems. In early 2008, Electionline.org held a series of meetings across the country for journalists and election officials. According to a report from Chicago, officials feel overwhelmed by the technological changes they have had to adapt to since 2000 and are discouraged by a lack of public confidence in voting.[37] Still, many said they were working hard to ensure 2008 would not be a repeat of Florida in 2000, or Ohio in 2004.

RESULTS MAY NOT BE KNOWN ON ELECTION NIGHT

November's election may well be a landslide and the next President of the United States will be known on Election Night. If it's a close contest, however, the winner may not be declared for several days, or even longer. Because of the vast numbers of people voting by mail (absentee) and the increased use of paper ballots,[38] some states will need extra time to count all the ballots. After California's February 5 primary, unofficial results were released, but it took several weeks for all of the ballots to be counted. Provisional ballots accounted for some of the delay, but a last-minute deluge of absentee ballots also slowed the counting. Los Angeles County aside, half of the state votes by mail.[39] And many states expect voting by mail to increase in the fall.

Introduction

California was hardly alone in this regard. In the Indiana primary on May 6, the country waited until past midnight local time for Lake County, home of the city of Gary, to report the final results in a tightening contest between Democrats Hillary Clinton and Barack Obama. County officials claimed the delay was caused by a record turnout of 133,000 voters, plus 11,000 early paper ballots (triple the number cast in 2004) that had to be counted by hand, as well as the time needed to collect electronic voting machine memory cards from polling places.[40]

> "Voters need to know what they can and cannot control. You can control your ability to register properly; verify your registration with local election officials; know what ID is required; and find out in advance the location of your polling place. You cannot control how well election machinery works or whether there will be a problem with the vote count."

Chastened local leaders promised they would do better next time. The day after the primary, Gary's mayor, Rudy Clay, declared the debacle would not be repeated and said he had already begun discussing changes with officials that would hasten ballot counting in November.[41] Meanwhile, observers such as CNN.com's Jeffrey Toobin suggested the delay was due in part to local politicians tinkering with the results.

With so many factors in play, voters need to know what they can and cannot control. You can control your ability to register properly; verify your registration with local election officials; know what ID is required; and find out in advance the location of your polling place. You cannot control how well election machinery works or whether there will be a problem with the vote count.

Looking ahead to November, we can focus on helping as many people as possible vote for the presidential candidate of their choice. That starts with being properly registered to vote (unless you live in North Dakota,

Introduction

which, unlike the other 49 states and the U.S. territories, has no voter registration). Unfortunately, throughout American history, voting has not been open to everyone. It took generations for those who did not own property, African Americans, Native Americans, women, and people younger than 21 to obtain the right to vote. Today, voting is open to all who register—yet an estimated 64 million Americans who are eligible to vote are *not* registered. That's nearly one-third of our nation's voting-age citizens.[42]

Chapter One
VOTER REGISTRATION

REGISTERING TO VOTE is supposed to be easy. You get a registration form from the post office or other government office; you fill it out and sign it; then you mail it or submit it in person at City Hall, the DMV, or the county office. Then you're all set. Right?

Well, *mostly*. Depending on your state, there are other important details you may have to find out for yourself, such as where you go to vote. Not every state or county sends postcards to new voters reminding them where their polling place is. States also expect new voters to bring certain types of ID to the polls. Indeed, any first-time voter who registers by mail must present identification at the polls. More experienced voters seeking to vote by mail (absentee), or wanting to vote early (before Election Day), have other rules to follow that we'll address later. For now, the process begins with being properly registered, and in the U.S. it is up to each individual, not the government, to ensure this is done correctly. The last thing you want is to wait in line to vote on November 4 only to discover you aren't properly registered or that your name is missing from local voter registration lists.

Chapter One

MISSING IN ACTION?

FOR YEARS, VOTER REGISTRATION ROLLS were maintained at the local level. County and township officials removed (or were supposed to remove) people who died, moved, or were convicted of felonies. But after the messy 2000 Florida election, Congress passed the Help America Vote Act of 2002 (HAVA), which not only helped states buy new electronic voting machines, but also required that every state keep a list of registered voters. While some states had those lists before HAVA, November 2008 will be the first presidential election for which all states are required to use statewide voter lists.[43]

> "November 2008 will be the first presidential election for which all states are required to use statewide voter lists. Unfortunately, the new lists are not always accurate."

Unfortunately, the new lists are not always accurate. Thousands of people who went to vote in the primaries discovered they were not listed, or were identified with a political party not of their choosing. Some states had hired private firms to prepare the lists, but whether the problem was outsourcing, data entry, dated state election records, or voter error is not clear, since election officials are reluctant to discuss the issue.[44] By early March, incorrect voter lists had already caused problems in New Mexico, Arizona, and California.[45] In early 2008 in Travis County, Texas, where the city of Austin is located, county officials discovered that 8,500 names were incorrectly removed when the statewide voter database came online in 2007.[46]

People whose names are not on polling place voter lists can request a provisional ballot, which was created by HAVA to ensure eligible voters can vote. But provisional ballots have to be verified before they are counted. That means they are not included in results released on Election Night.

Voter Registration

And in some states, a lot of provisional ballots are rejected if they do not include all the required information. In half the states, these ballots only count if they are turned in at the correct precinct.[47] That means voters have to make sure they are at the right location—or, in a multi-precinct polling place, possibly the correct table—for their vote to count.

But back to voter lists. Arizona,[48] New Mexico,[49] and Georgia[50] had problems of their own. Thousands of people in Phoenix and Tucson discovered their political party had been misidentified, or were told by poll workers that they had requested and received absentee ballots. In some cases, these were not errors and poll workers no doubt were right that some people had forgotten which party they had registered in or that they had requested an absentee ballot. But many voters told poll workers they were mistaken and were given a provisional ballot. While there could be many underlying causes for the mix-up, the way voters were listed on Arizona's new statewide rolls clearly deserved some of the blame.

New Mexico and Georgia had different data-related problems. In New Mexico, Democratic Party officials running their presidential caucus said the list provided by the state's Democratic secretary of state, Mary Herrera, was missing one entire county and also had voters missing in other counties.[51] Election Systems & Software, one of the country's largest election vendors, prepared that list. All told, more than 17,000 people, or about 12 percent of Democratic caucus goers, cast provisional ballots in New Mexico in February. That's a very high percentage. The contest between Democratic presidential candidates for that state's delegates came down to the provisional ballot count, which Hillary Clinton narrowly won. In 2004, George W. Bush beat John Kerry in the state by 6,000 votes, a much smaller number than the provisional ballots issued in the state's Democratic caucus.

Chapter One

Something else happened in Georgia's primary. While many election protection lawyers were worried Georgia's new photo ID law would discourage turnout among the poor, students, and elderly voters, it was actually the new statewide voter database that caused long lines and hours-long delays in several counties. Apparently, administrators did not buy enough computers for poll workers to check in voters using a new system of electronic poll books and statewide lists.[52] As a result, bottlenecks developed, while voting machines stood empty. (Georgia's Democratic Party filed another suit in late May seeking to overturn the ID law.[53])

These three states were by no means the only ones to experience such issues. In Washington, D.C., about 10,000 people found they were not listed on voter rolls or were not registered with a political party—so they were not able to vote.[54] And in Rhode Island, where it isn't possible to change one's party affiliation on Election Day, a "handful" of voters went to vote but were handed ballots from another party.[55]

These setbacks presented voters with a choice: staying at their polling place until the issue was resolved—or leaving without voting. Some voters did go home, according to news reports and complaints to voter hotlines.[56] Others told poll workers that election officials were wrong about their registrations and demanded a ballot to vote. Most were given provisional ballots, which in some states means people had to fill out additional forms and verify their identity using an ID or utility bill. In some cases, people had to wait while poll workers called county officials for instructions, although they eventually were able to vote. And in a few cases, people had to go home and get another ID and return.

No one expects to face such hurdles when voting. It's a good idea to throw a current electric bill in your bag or briefcase, or take an extra

> "Voters should stay at their polling place until issues are resolved instead of leaving without voting."

government-issue photo ID, such as a passport, with you to the polls—especially if your existing ID has expired. If something happens, you won't have to go home grumbling about bungled bureaucracy and how much time it takes to vote!

VOTER PURGES

BEING REMOVED—OR PURGED—FROM VOTER LISTS is another possibility, especially if you live in a state or county with a history of close elections and where partisans have made a lot of noise about "voter fraud," which is the mostly nonexistent threat of people posing as other voters.[57] In recent presidential races, such as Florida in 2000 and Ohio in 2004, tens of thousands of voters were removed from voter rolls without their knowledge. In Florida, the state hired a private company that erroneously matched names and addresses with felons from across the country.[58] Most states strip felons of their right to vote while incarcerated. Florida's pre-2000 purge was seen as benefiting Republicans, as most of the purged voters came from communities with recent histories of voting for Democrats. (See "Felon Voting," later in the chapter.)

In Cleveland, Ohio, between 2000 and 2004, the number of people who were purged from Cuyahoga County's voter lists was more than one-third of the number of people who voted for Al Gore for president in 2000.[59] In 2004, Ohio's Republican Party chairman headed that county's board of elections, which conducted the purge. Equally eyebrow-raising is that most Democratic campaign organizations that were bragging during the summer of 2004 about their voter registration efforts were not aware of the purges in Cleveland, Ohio's largest Democratic stronghold, or in other Ohio cities as late as that August.[60]

Chapter One

In 2008, an election commissioner in Madison County, Mississippi, single-handedly purged more than 10,000 voters—including a Republican congressional candidate and his wife. In the local uproar that followed, the names were put back on the books before the state's presidential primary.[61] In late March in Columbus-Muscogee County, Georgia, the county election office mailed 700 letters to voters saying they had been purged from voter lists because they had been convicted of felonies.[62] The American Civil Liberties Union said the error was due to Georgia's secretary of state comparing names from a variety of state databases.[63]

The full extent of voter purges in 2008 is not known. That is because the process of cleaning up voter lists is largely done behind closed doors or outsourced. Also, many states will be purging voters after the primaries and caucuses but before the fall election. While the process has legitimate goals, such as removing the names of people who move, die, or are convicted of felonies, there is room for errors, and affected voters could be in the dark come Election Day, unless they check to see if their voter registration is current.

Here's how it works. Typically, if a voter skips one federal election cycle—i.e., doesn't vote in a two-year period—local officials will send a "do not forward" postcard to verify their address. If the card is not returned, a voter is considered "inactive." Inactive voters can show up and vote like anybody else, without filling out new paperwork. But if a voter is on the inactive list for two federal election cycles—a four-year period—that voter can be purged. (Some counties, such as in rural Ohio, consider one federal election cycle to be four years, not two.[64]) In other words, if you haven't voted since the last presidential election, you should verify your registration is still valid.

> **"If you haven't voted since the last presidential election in 2004, make sure that your voter registration is still valid."**

Voter Registration

Critics say this process is unfair to poor people, students, and younger people, who tend to move more often than middle-class families with children or the elderly. They also say purges can have partisan implications if all jurisdictions are not treated equally. But the process is dictated in federal law. Under the National Voter Registration Act of 1993, states are required not just to compile new statewide voters lists but also to do "list maintenance"—or voter purges—to prepare those lists.

What makes 2008 different is that there are new pressures on the states to purge voters. First, there is HAVA's requirement to create statewide voter lists. But unlike past years when political parties pushed purges to gain an advantage by targeting the opposition's base, a big difference in 2008 is that the U.S. Department of Justice, which enforces the nation's voting laws, has been pressuring states to purge their voter lists.

In April 2007, the department's Voting Section sent letters to top election officials in 10 states—Iowa, Massachusetts, Mississippi, Nebraska, North Carolina, Rhode Island, South Dakota, Texas, Utah, and Vermont—pressuring them to do more purging.[65] Since 2005, the Voting Section has also sued six other states or jurisdictions—Indiana, Maine, Missouri, New Jersey, Philadelphia, and Pulaski County, Arkansas—and purging voter rolls was part of the resulting settlements.[66] Only Missouri fought a Voting Section suit, winning in federal court, although that decision has been appealed.

As of spring 2008, the scope of voter purges in most of these states was unknown. The state of Indiana purged 617,447 names between June 2006 and its May 2008 primary; a number equal to 12.5 percent of the state's registered voters.[67] Indiana officials said they had some of the most outdated voter rolls in the country before their purge,[68] while activists worried that eligible voters were being removed.[69] That state, and the others as well,

Chapter One

are likely to continue their list maintenance during the summer—after the primaries but before the fall election.

Removing voters from the rolls during a presidential season in which voter interest has been historic and turnout records have been set may seem odd, or it may seem political, an attempt to shape the electorate to one party's benefit. For the voter, the solution is simple: Just make sure you are properly registered to vote, and do not wait until October to do it. If you know people who have not voted in recent years who want to vote in 2008, tell them they must check their registration information or possibly re-register.

The simplest way to do this is to call your local election office—which usually is at the county or city level, although some rural states still run elections at the township level. Ask if you are on voter rolls, and confirm that you will be able to vote in November. Calling the local election board is critical, because it is legally responsible for administering the election. Advocacy groups do not have this legal status.

> **"** Calling local election officials to check your registration information is critical because they are legally responsible for registering voters and administering the election. Advocacy groups do not have this legal status. **"**

One great tool to speed your checking is a national directory of local election officials, which can be found on the Overseas Vote Foundation website (Overseasvotefoundation.org). The Election Official Directory contains detailed contact information for every jurisdiction in the country, including names, phone and fax numbers, e-mails, and office hours. One more tip: If you call, write down the name of the person you spoke with and take it to your polling place on Election Day. That way, if your registration is questioned, you can say, "Well, I recently talked to...."

Voter Registration

Why do this now, or sooner rather than later? First, it will be much easier to contact local election boards in the summer than in the fall to verify your information. Second, if for some reason you have to re-register, checking earlier means there is less likelihood your application will get lost as election officials plow through thousands of voter registrations turned in during late September or early October. One legitimate complaint election officials have is that organizers of too many voter registration drives dump thousands of applications at the last minute. Officials are hard-pressed to process them all and sometimes end up hiring temporary staff to input the data. Those temporary workers face tremendous workloads and can make data-entry mistakes. That's why acting sooner is better.

VOTER REGISTRATION: THE DETAILS

BEFORE YOU CAN VOTE, you have to register. Every state's top election administrator, whether a secretary of state or election board, has a website with registration forms and directions, contacts for local election officials (where forms often are to be submitted), and answers to most questions about the voting process. Some websites are bilingual.

> **"Don't wait until October to register to vote because 27 states cut off voter registration 20 or more days before the next election."**

There are plenty of websites and groups that can help you with this, from the League of Women Voters (www.lwv.org) to the Voter Education Network (www.nonprofitvote.org), whose homepage map lets you click on a state and retrieve registration and other information. There are excellent sites geared toward younger voters, such as www.DeclareYourself.com. The Overseas Voting Foundation (www.overseasvotefoundation.org) website helps civilian and military voters with filling out registration forms, and

Chapter One

its directory of local and state election officials is very useful with quickly finding the right person to answer your questions. At these websites, you also can get forms, find frequently asked questions, register in English or Spanish, etc.

There are three basic qualifications to register:
- you must be a U.S. citizen;
- you must be a resident of the state in which you are planning to register;
- you must be at least 18 years old at the time of the next election.

Residency means the home address where you live. You cannot have more than one residence for voter registration purposes. States vary on the minimum amount of time you need to have lived at that address before qualifying to register to vote. (See the State-by-State Voting Guide.)

Then there is the fine print:
- most states require that you not be imprisoned or on parole for a felony conviction;
- you cannot be mentally incompetent, as currently determined by a court;
- you have to register before your state's registration deadline, typically about a month before Election Day (which in 2008 is November 4). According to Demos.org, 27 states cut off voter registration 20 or more days before the next election. In some of these states, your first vote has to be in person—not by mail.

Voter Registration

SAME DAY REGISTRATION

NINE STATES—Idaho, Iowa, Maine, Minnesota, Montana, Nebraska, New Hampshire, Wisconsin, and Wyoming—have Election Day registration, which means you can show up, register, and vote. These states require identification, so be sure to take some with you—a government-issue photo ID, if possible. A tenth state, North Carolina, allows for same-day registration at early voting sites, usually county buildings. States allowing Election Day registration generally have voter turnouts that are as much as 10 percent or more above other states.

Most post offices have voter registration forms, which can be completed and mailed to election officials in your state. Forms are also available at motor vehicle departments, political campaign offices, and online at the website of the state's election department (see the State-by-State Voting Guide at the back of the book for website addresses). It is critical that you send the form to the right address. If you are a new state resident or a student, you'll probably have to provide a copy of a utility bill or bank statement to verify your new residence. Again, if you register by mail, you will have to present identification at your polling place. Some schools will print out a student phone bill with the dorm address (see Chapter Two for details).

In all states, if you are registering for the first time by mail, you will need to provide specific forms of identification at your polling place. The requirements can range from any government-issue photo ID to the last four digits of a Social Security number. Most states accept a driver's license or passport. Other forms of non-photo ID are acceptable, but they vary from state to state. You must check and understand the rules for your state. Wyoming, for example, wants people to register to vote in person. New Hampshire, in contrast, only accepts mail-in forms to request absentee ballots.

Chapter One

OTHER WAYS TO REGISTER

LIKE STATE MOTOR VEHICLE DEPARTMENTS, state welfare offices also are supposed to ask the public if they want to register to vote, according to the National Voter Registration Act (NVRA). But according to 2008 studies by advocacy groups like Project Vote, Demos, and the Association of Community Organizations for Reform Now (ACORN), many state social welfare agencies are not implementing the law, potentially affecting millions of lower-income Americans.[70] Some states are now being sued for this, but it is not clear whether litigation will be settled to affect registration before the 2008 election.

Veterans living in Department of Veterans Affairs hospitals or on VA campuses face other issues when it comes to registering to vote. After pressure from lawsuits and several U.S. senators urging the VA to become a NVRA registration agency, the VA announced in April that it would help hospitalized veterans to register and vote.[71] Less than two weeks later, the VA issued another directive saying it would help individual voters who asked for help but would not allow voter registration drives.[72] While it remains to be seen how, or if, the VA will implement the policy, if these veterans recently have moved they will lose their right to vote unless they re-register or update their registration information.

Certain states offer early voting before Election Day. Of course, you have to be registered to vote early. North Carolina will allow people to register and vote at early voting sites. And most states offer absentee ballots, or voting by mail, although there are varying rules for who qualifies for these ballots (See Chapter Three).

Finally, there is an emerging trend to watch in 2008: Some states are seeking to follow the lead of Arizona, which in 2004 began requiring proof of citizenship before a person could register to vote.[73] In February, the

Kansas City Star reported that Missouri was "among a dozen states this year" considering such a requirement. "Supporters say such a law is necessary because of what they think is a growing trend among illegal immigrants to register to vote," the paper reported. "Opponents see it as anti-Hispanic legislation that's a solution for a problem that doesn't exist."[74]

While the Missouri Legislature did not pass that bill in the 2008 session, the notion that more ballot security laws are needed is not going away. Requiring such proof is likely to complicate voting for a wider section of the public, according to a 2007 study,[75] which found more than half of married women do not have a new birth certificate with their married name on it. The study also reported that 7 percent of U.S. citizens, some 13 million people, particularly low-income people, "do not have ready access to citizenship documents."

As of June 1, bills with the proof of citizenship requirement to register were pending in California, Illinois, and Michigan, according to Project Vote. In early May, before their state legislatures adjourned, nine other states were considering similar bills.[76] Those measures died when those states ended their 2008 legislative sessions. In Virginia, a bill was signed into law that lets registrars remove "all persons known by him not to be United States citizens" from voter rolls unless they provide citizenship proof within two weeks of being contacted by mail. That could be a problem if registrars remove names and those people do not respond in time.

FELON VOTING

DISENFRANCHISEMENT, or denying people the right to vote, particularly affects people who have been convicted of a felony. According to the Sentencing Project, a nonprofit based in Washington, D.C., 5.3 million citizens lost the right to vote when they were convicted of a felony, including 1.4 million African American men and more than 675,000 women.

Only two states, Maine and Vermont, allow prisoners to vote while they are incarcerated. The rest of the states bar inmates from voting. Across the country there are many legal hurdles these people face to recover their right to vote. Thirteen other states and Washington, D.C., allow ex-felons to regain the right to vote after their prison terms. The remaining states have policies that permit renewed voting depending upon the crime, completion of probation, and payment of fines. In some states, the process is difficult.[77]

Ex-felons need to determine if they are eligible to vote in their state. SentencingProject.org has a chart of state laws ex-felons should review before calling local election boards to register, since local election officials are not always aware of the specifics of this area of the law. The Sentencing Project does not advocate for individuals, but assistance is available from the League of Women Voters as well as many state and local chapters of the ACLU.

Ex-felon enfranchisement is an area in which would-be voters need to know their rights and be willing to possibly educate election officials—an awkward role to be sure. However, helping former offenders rejoin mainstream society is a worthy goal that no one can argue against.

SUMMING UP

CLEARLY, THERE ARE QUITE A VARIETY of voter registration rules across the nation. Same-day registration is easiest, but most states are more concerned that people meet and can document basic criteria. Whether or not that's fair, the solution lies in knowing the rules in your state and satisfying them. You may be confident that you are qualified to vote, but if you want to participate in the next presidential election, or any election, you must

Voter Registration

still compile the necessary paperwork if you live in a state that demands such a record.

Hang on to the documents you use to register, or make copies, so come Election Day you have a folder of paperwork you can grab on your way to the polls. If you are among the few who run into database errors, missing registration information, incorrect voter purges, or any other obstacle—including political party volunteers challenging your registration—you will be prepared to prove that you are a legal, registered voter.

> **"If you want to vote, you must compile the necessary paperwork to register and bring the correct ID to your polling place."**

The 866-OUR-VOTE hotlines will be available well before Election Day. You can also ask almost any political campaign or campaign volunteer for help, although be forewarned: you should expect to get calls urging you to vote for their candidate or cause.

Chapter Two
STUDENT VOTING

For years, conventional wisdom held that young people were not interested in voting. In recent presidential elections, turnout among all age groups has hovered between 50 and 60 percent, which actually is below most other Western democracies. Within the low turnout in the United States, the trend for people aged 18 to 29 has been even lower. In 2006, only 22 percent of eligible voters from this age group voted.[78]

APATHETIC NO MORE

THE STATUS QUO IS CHANGING IN 2008. Younger people have been drawn to political campaigns—volunteering, contributing, and voting—in a manner not seen in generations.[79] According to the Student Association for Voter Empowerment (SaveVoting.org), youth who are engaged in politics are more likely to vote.[80] Exit polls reported that the high turnout in many of the 2008s primaries was due in part to increased youth voting.

It hasn't always been apathy that has discouraged many young people, but the intimidating system of hurdles they must often clear before voting. Former undergraduates who waited for more then 10 hours to vote at Ohio's

Chapter Two

Kenyon College in 2004 founded SaveVoting.org. As a 2004 report from the League of Conservation Voters put it, "Students face structural barriers to student voting and targeted voter suppression."[81] The league's report cited restrictive residency requirements, confusing absentee ballot rules, voter intimidation at the polls, voter suppression tactics, and a lack of nearby polling places.

> **"**Registering to vote isn't the only obstacle students face. In November 2004, Kenyon College students infamously waited in line until after midnight because Knox County officials had only one working voting machine at the liberal arts college.**"**

Many states still have rules that discourage students from voting. The Student Public Interest Research Group's New Voter Project, which has helped 600,000 students register since 2003, studied two of these states—Arizona and New Mexico—in the 2006 election cycle. "In Arizona, those wanting to register to vote were required to provide an Arizona drivers' license or identification card," the *Harvard Crimson* reported.[82] Students without these IDs were asked to show a birth certificate or a passport—not the kinds of documents that out-of-state students typically carry with them, the PIRG study noted. In contrast, no form of ID was required to register to vote in Massachusetts, home of the *Crimson*.

In New Mexico, the barriers were subtler. Most groups conducting voter registration drives, including those targeting students, "were required to submit an oath saying they would follow all election laws and were only permitted to have a limited number of voter registration forms in their possession at a time," the *Crimson* reported.[83] Needless to say, the more complicated the registration process, the fewer its volunteers.

The difficulties of obtaining the newly required state photo ID card—typically a driver's license—were also apparent in Indiana's November 2007 election, where two editors from the Purdue University newspaper

Student Voting

were prevented from voting while trying to follow the state's new voter ID law.[84] Students trying to get Indiana IDs were forced to leap bureaucratic hurdles when the motor vehicles bureau rejected their out-of-state documents. Just before that state's May 6 primary, Indiana newspapers were reporting that different counties had varying policies on whether student IDs were acceptable.[85]

During the 2008 primary, poll workers told students at Notre Dame, Butler University, and St. Mary's College that they lacked the required IDs.[86] While Indiana poll workers were undoubtedly just doing their job and following state law, that example underscores why it is so important that students understand the law in their state.

Registering to vote isn't the only obstacle students face. In November 2004, Kenyon College students infamously waited in line until after midnight because Knox County officials had only one working voting machine at the liberal arts college. Those same officials deployed more than a half-dozen voting machines to a nearby Christian school where there was no wait to vote.[87]

In the days before the 2008 Iowa caucuses, the state's largest paper and several Democratic presidential campaigns strongly suggested that out-of-state students refrain from participating, implying they would dilute the vote of longtime Iowans.[88] In late February 2008, more than 1,000 students at Texas' Prairie View A&M University marched seven miles to protest that county officials would not open an early voting center on campus for the state's March 4 primary.[89] The protest was not the first in Prairie View concerning student voting. The county responded by opening additional early voting sites for the primary, although the closest site to campus was a mile away.

None of these hurdles are insurmountable. If millions of young people want to have a voice in the issues that matter to them, all they have to do is treat the registration process like a tedious homework assignment; it may take a little time, but the payoff is worth it.

STUDENT REGISTRATION

IT WASN'T SO LONG AGO that young people lacked the right to vote. The Twenty-sixth Amendment, which lowered the national voting age to 18, was ratified in 1971 after soldiers drafted in the Vietnam War argued that if they were old enough to fight, they were old enough to vote.

In 1979, the U.S. Supreme Court ruled that students could vote where they went to school as long as they established residency. The court did not define "residency," leaving that to state legislatures. While bowing to local control is a political tradition as old as the nation, it also creates separate and unequal standards across the United States. Many state and local officials did not want students voting in their communities, fearing their numbers could overwhelm local politics. The tactics these bureaucrats used could be described as contemporary versions of the barriers thrown at minorities throughout American history. "Officials have created residency questionnaires, much like the literacy tests of yore, specifically targeted at students, rejected registration forms from dorms, and made empty threats that students will forfeit financial aid or their child dependency status when they switch their registration information," the *American Prospect* noted.[90]

On the other hand, the opportunity for students to vote is broader than it has been at any other time in the nation's history.[91] You just have to follow the necessary steps: present the proper identification when registering to vote, usually a government-issue photo ID and/or a utility bill with an address on it. Some schools, such as Oberlin College in Ohio, have made the process easier by working with their local county election board.

Student Voting

Oberlin prints a special phone bill for students that lists their address and satisfies Ohio's voter ID requirement.[92]

But not every school facilitates the voting process for its students. A 2004 Harvard University study "found 33 percent of American colleges and universities—and 44 percent of private institutions—are not in compliance with 1998 amendments to the Higher Education Act that requires schools receiving federal funding to provide students with a mail-in voter registration form."[93]

DeclareYourself.org offers this advice for students who live in a dorm and use a school mailbox or receive mail at a P.O. Box:[94] "If you receive mail in a post office box, you can sign an affidavit or get a letter from your college's Residential Life office, asserting you live at your dorm's address. If you have a post office box as your permanent address, your voter registration form will not be processed. There is a section on the voter registration form to put your mailing address, in addition to your physical address."

Students studying abroad can have their ballots sent to their foreign address. See Overseasvotefoundation.org to register to vote and request a ballot and to look up election deadlines state by state.

THE REALITY FOR 2008

YOU HAVE THE CHOICE of establishing residency where you attend school, or registering to vote by mail in the community where your parents live. While the latter may seem easier, because you probably got your driver's license in your hometown, it's actually not that difficult to use the same IDs to register where you go to school. Some states, including Illinois, Louisiana, Michigan, Nevada, Tennessee, Virginia, and West Virginia,[95] do not permit first-time voters to vote by mail (absentee). And that's not the only absentee ballot fine print. Some states allow absentee ballot requests

Chapter Two

online and others do not; some states require these requests be made shortly before the election and need witnesses or a notary. And many states require separate applications for absentee ballots for both the primary and the general (or fall) election.

Basically, you must have the required documentation, and make sure your application is properly filled out and submitted in time. If you need help, it would be worth a quick trip to your local city or county offices, or ask someone working on voter registration. They can also tell you how to find your polling place. Save your paperwork and bring it with you on Election Day.

> **"If you need help registering, it would be worth a quick trip to your local city or county offices. They can also tell you how to find your polling place. Save your paperwork and bring it with you on Election Day."**

High school students who will be 18 by November 4, 2008, need to pay special attention to the rules. In late April, election officials in Montgomery County, Maryland wrote to some teenagers who will turn 18 before the November election informing them they could not vote in earlier elections in 2008. While the recipients felt they had lost their right to vote, the bureaucratic response was correct, as those individuals would not be of age yet.[96]

Finally, when registering, ask if your state allows early voting. This option usually means going to a county office building to vote in person. Voting with an absentee ballot before the election may also be an option. In both cases, voting before Election Day often helps people avoid long lines.

Chapter Three
ABSENTEE VOTING

MANY VOTERS DO NOT WANT to wait in line on Election Day, while others prefer to study ballots in the privacy of their own homes before they make their selections. For elderly or disabled people, soldiers stationed overseas, and citizens living abroad, voting by mail is a necessity if they want to vote at all. Students also may choose to vote by mail instead of registering where they go to school. As a result of these trends, absentee voting, or voting by mail, is becoming increasingly popular. In California, absentee ballots accounted for half of the ballots cast in the fall 2006 election, if you take Los Angeles County out of the equation.[97] That number is only expected to rise in 2008.

All states allow voters to vote by mail, but there is wide variation on who is eligible to receive an absentee ballot. The process of registering to vote and requesting an absentee ballot can be complicated. In many states there is a window during which

> **All states allow voters to vote by mail, but there is wide variation on who is eligible to receive an absentee ballot.**

you must request a ballot, usually in the month or weeks before Election Day. Most states also require that the ballots be returned before the polls close on Election Day. In some states, voters can turn absentee ballots in at their precincts on Election Day. Like all voting rules, the law varies by state.

Voting by mail has its ups and downs. If you vote absentee, there is a small chance your ballot will not be counted by the time the "unofficial" tallies are announced on Election Night, although your ballot will be counted before the vote total is certified. This is because as more people vote by mail and most of those ballots come in at the last minute, election officials are not always able to count all the ballots by the time Election Night results, however incomplete, are released to the media.

In November 2006, 20 percent of California's mail-in ballots were uncounted by midnight on Election Day. After the state's 2008 primary in February, some 600,000 absentee ballots and 400,000 provisional ballots remained to be counted—equal to the number of Democratic votes cast in Virginia.[98] Should the election in your state be close, this could be a factor in the projected winners announced by the media.

Some voters have no choice but to vote by mail, namely homebound seniors, the disabled, and people overseas. For infirm seniors and people with disabilities, there are two issues. The first is getting the ballot, which usually entails having someone help with completing an absentee ballot application after the voter has registered to vote. The second concerns voting and mailing the absentee ballot. There have been documented cases of unscrupulous campaigners telling people how to vote instead of merely aiding with the process.[99] This has led some experts to say voting by mail is more susceptible to vote fraud or padding vote totals than precinct-based voting.[100]

Those who vote absentee must ensure their ballots are returned on time. In some states, such as Texas, it's a crime for anybody who is not a family member to carry or mail another person's absentee ballot, unless they sign their name on the envelope. While the Texas attorney general has been prosecuting these cases since 2004, critics say they target longtime Democratic Party volunteers who have a tradition of helping their elderly neighbors vote.[101] In May, the attorney general settled a lawsuit challenging these prosecutions, and he agreed to end this tactic.[102] It remains to be seen how that settlement will affect the 2008 campaign.

For overseas voters, especially members of the military, registering and requesting an absentee ballot is only half the challenge. These voters must receive and return their ballots in time so they can be counted. With the unpredictable speed of overseas delivery, this is no small hurdle. Also, in a few states, such as New Mexico and Mississippi, the registration and filing deadlines for overseas civilians is not the same as for members of the military.[103] The Department of Defense, which oversees military voting, has worked with 20 states to create a system under which ballots can be faxed in. However, some election lawyers are critical of that process, saying it eliminates a secret ballot because officers will know how their soldiers voted.[104] The soldiers must first sign waivers saying they understand their ballots are not secret.[105]

Another downside of voting by mail is the increased chance of voters making errors that will void their vote. If you make a mistake at a polling place, you can ask for another ballot. The most common errors when voting by mail include voting for more than one candidate in a race, sending in the ballot late, failing to use the right postage, not including the right identification, and not signing in the correct place.[106]

There are still many advantages to voting by mail. It may increase turnout by as much as 4 or 5 percent in fall and local elections, according to one study.[107] (That increase tends to be among middle-class and older voters.) Common Cause, an election reform group, lists these pluses: It can reduce the potential for delays and long lines at the polls; it can increase the

Chapter Three

opportunity for get-out-the-vote campaigns; and it can offset the impact of negative political ads, because those tend to occur in the final days of a race, after people send in their ballots. Voting by mail also reduces election costs and the need for trained poll workers.[108]

STEPS TO TAKE

THERE ARE THREE STEPS to voting by mail: registering, requesting a ballot, and voting. The process may seem a bit complicated, but plenty of online help is available.

To start, you have to be registered to vote and have a legal voting residence in a state or territory. For most people, this means registering to vote where they live. For citizens who are overseas, this means registering in the last place they lived in the states or a territory, even if they have been abroad for many years. For soldiers who are overseas, this means their address of domicile. Veterans living at VA campuses will have to register using those locations as their new address.

> "There are three steps to voting by mail: registering, requesting a ballot, and voting. There is plenty of online help available."

OVERSEAS VOTERS

FOR ALL OVERSEAS CITIZENS, the voter registration/ballot request form is a single application that simultaneously performs both functions. Traditionally, it has been called the "federal postcard application form" (FPCA, SF 76), although it is not a postcard at all. It is a form that is nationally accepted and must be completed and sent to the proper election office

Absentee Voting

in the states. State deadlines vary widely, but you can look them up in the Voter Information Directory on Overseasvotefoundation.org.

If you will be overseas for the election, file your application form as soon as possible. Most states require that it be received 30 days prior to the election, but that's really waiting until the last minute because overseas ballots usually are sent out by then. Be sure to include an e-mail address on the form so your local election official can contact you in case of questions.

Members of the military can use online services such as Military.overseasvotefoundation.org, which automates the registration and ballot request process, or they can request help from a voting assistance officer in their unit, according to the Pentagon's 2008–09 Voting Assistance Guide.[109] Soldiers overseas should register by August 15 of the election year, while those who are active-duty and based in the states should register by September 15. But earlier is always better. While some states have laws allowing for late registrations by soldiers returning from deployments or leaving the military, there is no uniform policy. Any time a soldier or veteran (or anyone else) changes location, they have to re-file their voter registration/ballot request form that also serves as a change-of-address form.

The military's Voting Assistance Guide lists these common mistakes when registering: not signing the form; failing to provide a complete voting address, or address where the ballot is to be sent; sending the registration form to the wrong voting jurisdiction; not selecting a political party (which will block voting in primary elections); mailing the form too late; giving no date of birth; and not having the form witnessed or notarized, if required.[110] Whether or not you are in the military, these mistakes can slow the registration process and make it hard to correct later on.

The registration process is daunting for citizens or soldiers overseas, but new online tools vastly simplify the process. The Overseas Vote

Chapter Three

Foundation's website guides voters through a series of question-and-answer windows, and in 10 minutes or less they can print their absentee voter application. Preparing that application is the hardest part of the process. The OVF tool, which secretaries of state in Alabama, Kentucky, Minnesota, Ohio, and West Virginia have licensed for use in 2008, also prints clear instructions on submitting the absentee ballot application. In 2008, OVF and Federal Express will team up to assist overseas and military voters in the speedy return of their ballots. The Express Your Vote program will run from September 15 through October 31, 2008. Details will be provided on the OVF and FedEx websites starting in early July. Automatic confirmation of ballot delivery to the election office is an invaluable benefit of this new service.

> "The Nonprofit Voter Engagement Network (Nonprofitvote.org) allows people to click on their state and request absentee ballot applications. The Overseas Vote Foundation's (Overseasvotefoundation.org) directory of election officials has names, e-mail addresses, phone numbers, and mailing addresses. These are the best online resources to use."

DOMESTIC VOTERS

DOMESTIC REGISTERED VOTERS must contact their county or state election office and request an absentee ballot. This can be done in person at county election offices or by mail. The Nonprofit Voter Engagement Network (Nonprofitvote.org) allows people to click on their state and request absentee ballot applications. It also has instructions on how to submit those forms. Their website should be very useful for seniors. The OVF site's directory of election officials has names, e-mail addresses, phone numbers, and mailing addresses. Applications may be available online at secretaries

Absentee Voting

of state websites, and some states even attach them to sample ballots sent out before an election. Some states, such as California, allow registered voters to become "permanent vote-by-mail voters," meaning they will not have to reapply for absentee ballots.[111]

What if your ballot doesn't arrive? The first step, for domestic voters, is to call the county election office and ask why you have not received your ballot. This is important; in some states, like Pennsylvania, people who were listed as absentee voters but showed up to vote at their former local precinct were not allowed to cast ballots in the primary. Nobody wants to be in that situation in November.

If you are overseas and your ballot has not arrived by October of the election year, you can request a Federal Write-In Absentee Ballot (FWAB, SF 186), although this will only cover voting for president, vice president, U.S. senator, U.S. representative, delegate, or resident commissioner in the November election. Overseasvotefoundation.org automates this process as well. A handful of states accept this ballot as both a registration form and ballot.[112] You can also find valuable information on the Pentagon's website (fvap.gov), which has improved since 2004.[113]

Overseas ballots must be postmarked by Election Day to be counted. In some states, like Kansas, they must be *received* by Election Day to be counted; in other states, such as Florida, they can be received 10 days later. New York and Washington, D.C. will accept them up to two weeks after the election.[114]

There is one other development that might increase turnout from overseas and military voters, although from a security and accuracy standpoint, this option may be weaker than paperless voting machines. Thirteen states—Colorado, Delaware, Florida, Illinois (only some counties), Indiana, Mississippi, Montana, North Dakota, Oregon, South Carolina, Virginia, Washington, and Wisconsin—will send blank ballots to soldiers

Chapter Three

via e-mail.[115] Only seven of these states will allow the ballots to be returned by e-mail: Colorado, Indiana, Mississippi, Montana, North Dakota, South Carolina, and Washington. The other states require that ballots be returned via regular mail.

Chapter Four
VOTING MACHINES AND ELECTION OFFICIALS

THE WIDESPREAD INTRODUCTION of paperless electronic voting machines after the 2000 presidential election—when the nation watched and waited as Florida's computer punch-card ballots were examined, debated and recounted—has easily been the most controversial story in U.S. elections in recent years.

No voting system is perfect. All have problems that can affect how people vote and the accuracy of the ensuing vote count. Throughout American history every change in voting technology has been contentious—even the decision to stop voting in public and cast a secret ballot. But the scope of the machine breakdowns and tabulation errors with the latest generation of e-voting machines that have replaced paper ballots and ballot boxes has been far-reaching.

> **"**Throughout American history every change in voting technology has been contentious—even the decision to stop voting in public and cast a secret ballot. But the scope of the machine breakdowns and tabulation errors with the latest generation of e-voting machines has been far-reaching.**"**

Chapter Four

The primary concern with these systems is that there is no way to verify the accuracy of software-generated vote tallies or recount ballots in close contests. In 2004 dozens of voters in Youngstown, Ohio, reported voting for one presidential candidate while seeing the machine record a vote for his opponent. Poll workers dismissed their concerns and kept the machines in use.[116] Two years later, the same model of machine was used in Sarasota, Florida, where an estimated 15,000 votes in a congressional race vanished and were never recovered. (And more than 3,000 other votes were not recorded from voters who used paper ballot systems or voted absentee.) Republican Vern Buchanan was elected over Democrat Christine Jennings by fewer than 400 votes in Sarasota.

Dan Rather, the ex-CBS television anchorman now with HDNet, reported in mid-2007 that the voting machines used in Sarasota had touch-screen problems likely caused by shoddy overseas manufacture of the screen elements.[117] Other investigations by government officials, including Congress, found no clear consensus on what happened. Local election officials said the machines worked, but voters did not use them properly. Critics said the technology erred and lost data for which there was no paper-trail backup.[118] The point is that paperless systems do not offer a means of recovery, unlike their paper-based counterparts.

There were other problems reported with paperless technology. In Ohio in 2004, there were instances of thousands of votes *added* to the results after the polls closed. In one case covered by the media, in a polling place in a fundamentalist church in Columbus, the error was quickly corrected. What happened in Miami County, Ohio—19,000 votes were added to results after the polls closed—has never been fully explained.[119] Examples like these have led to criticisms that the machines are not only hampered by accuracy issues, but are also vulnerable to meddling with vote counts.

Voting Machines and Election Officials

More e-voting problems occurred during the 2008 primaries. In South Carolina's Republican primary, 80 percent of the voting machines in Horry County, where Myrtle Beach is located, failed to operate at the start of voting.[120] County officials blamed other county workers for the errors. In Pennsylvania, paperless machines also did not turn on at the start of voting, causing lines and delays.[121] In New Jersey, the electronic vote totals did not match the number of people who signed in to vote.[122] And in a few states in other parts of the all-electronic voting system, names of registered voters were missing from new statewide voter databases, which caused delays and forced voters to use provisional ballots.

Despite such accounts, electronic voting will be a large part of the landscape in November. Warren Stewart, of the advocacy group VerifiedVoting.org, projects that more than 25 percent of the public will be voting on electronic machines in more than 40,000 precincts across 14 states, including New Jersey, Virginia, and Pennsylvania.[123] Curiously, despite their track record and activists' concerns, voters apparently prefer electronic machines for their ease of use, even though some brands have error rates that can change outcomes in close elections.[124] Poll workers interviewed in Ohio during the 2008 primary said they preferred paperless machines because they were easier to use than paper-based voting.[125]

So far, e-voting's record in 2008 has not been as dire as many have predicted. No primary saw thousands of vanishing votes like Sarasota in 2006, or thousands of last-minute votes added, like Miami County, Ohio, in 2004. The problems that came to light apparently did not reverse the results of high-turnout elections. They were more sporadic and of a smaller scale and were related to election management issues.

Unfortunately, this record—determined from press reports, activist listservs and voter hotline logs—does not mean the November vote will be smooth sailing. The technology's capacity for error is unpredictable and on

Chapter Four

a larger scale than older, paper-based systems. The same e-voting system that was used in Sarasota will be in use in many states during the presidential vote, said VerifiedVoting's Stewart, which leaves open the possibility, however slim, of a repeat performance.

DIFFERENT COMPUTER VOTING SYSTEMS

THE DETAILS OF COMPUTER VOTING can be complicated, but you don't need to be a technology whiz to understand the process. The same lack of uniformity that makes the nation a patchwork of state and county election jurisdictions with varying rules and procedures also applies to voting machines and the related systems that keep election records, such as voters' names, addresses, signatures, and polling locations.

When it comes to voting systems, there actually are only a few varieties, each using different technologies. In a small number of rural locations, people mark paper ballots that are counted by hand. Far more common are the two other kinds of voting systems: one uses a paper ballot marked by a voter and counted by computer scanner; and the second uses a computer touch-screen or other interface that records votes electronically. Approximately one-quarter of these machines use older technology such as push buttons or dials, although the votes are still recorded by software.[126]

The optical-scan system, in which people mark their ballot with a pen and a computer scanner then reads the ballot, has been around since the 1970s. Increasingly, states with concerns about newer, paperless systems, such as Florida, California, Iowa, Colorado, and Ohio, have been returning to optical-scan systems before the November election. These systems are not trouble-free—scanners can read stray ink marks as votes[127] and optical scanners have been known to make tabulation errors.[128] What makes these systems preferable, many voting rights advocates say, is that paper ballots can be counted by hand in audits and recounts, and the voter's intent will be clear. Paperless systems do not provide that option.

With direct-recording electronic (DRE) machines, people touch a computer screen or other interface to vote, much as they use a bank ATM to withdraw money. On these systems, computer memory cards, similar to those used in digital cameras, have replaced the paper ballot and ballot boxes. Memory cards are then brought to central counting locations, usually county election offices, where precinct tallies are compiled electronically. (Optical scan systems also use memory cards and central counting; however, these systems retain paper ballots marked by voters.)

Responding to the criticism, manufacturers of some DRE systems have added a paper printout for voters to verify before casting their vote electronically. However, these add-on printers have not always worked in recent elections, prompting a growing number of academics, voting rights lawyers, and election officials to advocate their replacement with paper-based systems.[129]

Often, precincts will contain a mix of paper-based and electronic voting systems. In California, where the secretary of state has ordered county officials to return to optical-scan systems, there still is one DRE per precinct for voters with disabilities. In Ohio, where the secretary of state is pushing counties to return to optical-scan machines, some county officials are resisting. In that state's 2008 primary, the secretary also insisted these precincts have backup paper ballots;[130] however, many poll workers did not tell voters they had the option of voting on paper.[131]

Voters can make sure their e-voting machines are working properly. The websites of many secretaries of state now have demos of voting machines so voters can get a visual preview of touch-screen voting. VerifiedVoting.org has a web-based tool that allows voters to identify the

Chapter Four

type of voting machines used in almost every county in the U.S., along with contact information for local election officials.

On Election Day, if you believe a machine is malfunctioning, you should stop and ask a poll worker for help before casting your ballot. If the problem persists, ask to use another machine. If you experience the same problem on a second DRE machine, ask to vote on a backup paper ballot, call a voter hotline for help (1-866-OUR-VOTE), and talk to a lawyer or trained staffer. You also can call the campaign office of the presidential candidate you support, since campaigns station observers in polling places. If your voting system has a VVPAT printer attached, you should verify that your vote is correctly recorded before submitting your ballot. Voters should use common sense and remember that voting is a right, not a privilege. Poll workers are there to help you—as long as they follow their state's election laws.

> "If you believe a machine is malfunctioning, stop and ask a poll worker for help before casting your ballot. If the problem persists, ask to use another machine. If you experience the same problem on a second voting machine, ask for a backup paper ballot and call a voter hotline for help."

Unfortunately, some older DRE systems are designed in such a way that if a voter presses a candidate's name more than once, the machine deselects—or cancels—the vote. Many people in 2004 in states such as New Mexico were not aware of that feature, and double-pushed buttons, probably to make sure their choice was recorded. They did not realize they were erasing their vote! Ask a poll worker to see if this could be an issue in your precinct.

Voting Machines and Election Officials

VOTING OFFICIALS

MOST VOTERS WILL NEVER MEET the elected officials or county employees who run elections and buy the voting systems. Voters interact with poll workers and precinct judges, who are responsible for setting up and opening the polls, checking in voters and supervising the voting, assisting people with disabilities, and turning in the results.[132]

Poll workers are ordinary citizens doing a time-consuming and tedious job. Many have been at it for years, and untold thousands across the nation do a fine job. While they undergo regular training, some are not always as competent as the public would like. The fine points of using the newest voting systems or enforcing the newest laws account for many of the "competency" complaints that voter hotlines receive during the primary season.[133] It is important for voters, especially in a high-turnout election, to take a deep breath and be patient and polite if problems arise.

If a member of another political party challenges a voter's registration—which has been a Republican threat in recent presidential elections and is legal in battleground states such as Ohio and Indiana—keeping one's cool will encourage poll workers to fairly settle the matter. If your voter registration is correct and up to date, you have nothing to worry about. The goal of such challenges is as much to create bottlenecks and delays (in the hopes that frustrated people will leave without voting) as it is to validate voters' credentials.[134] That partisan tactic is an unfortunate residue of the era in

> **"** If a member of another political party challenges a voter's registration, keeping one's cool will encourage poll workers to fairly settle the matter. If your voter registration is correct and up to date, you have nothing to worry about. **"**

Chapter Four

the American South when the governing class sought to minimize minority voter turnout.

Still, staying calm and collected when your vote appears jeopardized is sometimes easier said than done. Consider this call to 1-866-MYVOTE1 during Indiana's May 6 primary:

> Hi. I just went in to vote. They wanted to see my drivers' license for identification purposes. And since my address did not match my current district, I felt like a criminal. I was made to sit aside for 15 minutes, until they made the appropriate phone call to find out the only thing that had to be required was that I had (photo) identification, not that I had to have the right address. It worked out, but it took 15 to 20 minutes. I still felt like a criminal. The people there don't have any idea what they are doing.[135]

This fellow did get to vote. While Indiana's tricky photo ID requirement was probably explained in a handout the poll workers received, the workers apparently did not understand the fine print. Fortunately, they figured it out, and the voter was not disenfranchised. Every election has moments like this. There will be more in November.

In another call, from North Carolina's May 6 primary, the voter also felt unfairly treated by poll workers; but again, the person did get to vote:

> I am calling about my husband's ballot being held up for processing. Even though there has been a resolution as to what was at question, and the chief official held onto it for about 10 to 15 minutes, and extended his time more than three times what it took someone else to vote at the polling site. We are a minor-

ity at this polling site. We are of mixed heritage, and it is a very Caucasian precinct.[136]

The lesson here is that knowing your rights and being patient with the process can go a long way toward ensuring you get to vote. Various advocacy groups, such as AdvancementProject.org and the Lawyers' Committee for Civil Rights Under Law (Lawyerscommittee.org) have online "know your rights" documents for various states. As for the poll workers in these examples, it's almost certain they would not detain voters with those particular issues again on that Election Day.

As we know, 2008's extended Democratic presidential contest has set turnout records for primary elections from coast to coast. Yet in state after state, officials looked at turnout statistics from the past few years to order supplies, such as the number of paper ballots, for their state's primary. That is why certain counties, such as Alameda County, California, where Oakland is located, ran out of ballots in some polls.[137] In Maryland's primary in February, bad weather and a shortage of paper ballots prompted the courts to order polls be kept open for an additional 90 minutes.[138] The emergence of these problems in the primary season has not gone unnoticed by election officials; many have pledged to be better prepared for the November election.

Poll workers, like their supervisors in county and state government, make mistakes. There is no reason to recount them all here. But there are several trends that could affect turnout in the fall. In addition to the challenges with new voter databases, electronic poll books, and new voting machines, some states are moving to what is known as voting centers—they are consolidating local polling stations into multi-precinct or regional voting hubs. Kansas[139] and Indiana are seeking to expand this way of voting, creating one center for every 10,000 voters in Indiana,[140] for example. New

Chapter Four

York is also considering consolidating polling stations in rural counties to save money.[141]

Election officials like the vote center idea because it saves money and requires fewer poll workers. Voters, however—especially those without cars—can have a difficult time getting to voting centers, and people who are used to voting close to home are sometimes unaware that their polling place has been moved. In Utah County, Utah, where Provo is located, the election supervisor was demoted after the public had difficulties finding where to vote after polling places were consolidated for the February primary.[142] The responsibility falls on voters to know where they are supposed to vote. Some states and counties print new poll locations on election guides, and many state election websites have polling place locator tools. But others do not, so voters must find out on their own. Consult Overseasvotefoundation.org's Election Official Directory to get an answer before Election Day.

> **If last-minute questions arise, two hotlines are available to help: 1-866-OUR-VOTE** connects callers to a lawyer or a trained volunteer, and **1-866-MYVOTE1** offers precinct location information and allows callers to leave a message for local election officials.

The other concern about voting centers is that voters need to be sure and stand in the correct line when they arrive. Voters should know their precinct number and ask to be certain they're in the right place—otherwise they may have to wait in line all over again. Also, in some states, such as Ohio, a voter who receives a provisional ballot must turn it in at the correct precinct—which can be one of several tables in a room. Before 2004, Ohio voters could turn in provisional ballots anywhere in their county.[143]

If last-minute questions arise, two hotlines are available to help: 1-866-OUR-VOTE connects callers to a lawyer or a trained volunteer, and

Voting Machines and Election Officials

1-866-MYVOTE1 offers precinct location information and allows callers to leave a message for local election officials. (Don't forget to leave your name, address, and telephone number so voter advocates or election officials can call you back.) Staffers report that most of the calls received concern registration information and poll location. Both hotlines also contact the media to publicize problems and alert voters.

On some occasions, it might be necessary to notify the local board of election or election administrator's office to try to rectify a problem. Should a problem require court intervention, a judge will first ask if all other avenues have been explored. It is not uncommon in these circumstances for local election officials, through their lawyers, to claim they never received any complaints.[144]

Chapter Five
ELECTION DAY REMINDERS/GETTING INVOLVED

ELECTION DAY

BY NOW YOU UNDERSTAND SEVERAL THINGS: the need to be properly registered; to know the location of your polling place and its precinct number (unless you're voting by mail); and to bring the required voter ID to the polls. You know to give yourself plenty of time to vote (and to wait in line) on November 4; and should any registration questions arise, you know you can advocate for your right to get a regular ballot. You should also know that if you're waiting in line at the close of polling hours, you are legally allowed to vote, even if you will be casting your ballot after the poll closes.

It is possible that the credentials of a small number of people may be challenged, either by poll workers or by campaign volunteers representing one political party. Partisan voter challenges are legal in many states, even though in 2004 they tended to be the subject of pre-election threats rather than actual occurrences at the polls.[145] The law for challenges varies from state to state. In some states, they are legal only if the challenger knows the voter and has actual knowledge that he or she resides elsewhere.

Chapter Five

Should you be the subject of an election challenge, there are several things you can do. First, be reassured that if your registration is up to date, you *will* get to vote. Besides tolerating the delay and showing the correct ID to poll workers, you should call 1-866-OUR-VOTE, and you will be connected to an attorney. You should also call the local offices of the presidential candidate you are supporting. Calls to political party offices or campaign offices will also bring assistance, as both prepare for this possibility.

As always, the solution to this and most other scenarios that can impede voting is to check your registration information and poll location information well before Election Day. Typically it's voters who have recently moved or registered—especially students—who are targets for voter challenges since they are not as familiar with election procedures.

GETTING MORE INVOLVED

THERE ARE NUMEROUS OPTIONS if you want to get more involved in the voting process or if you want to volunteer for a political party, candidate, or activist group.

First, contact your local election office (town clerk, city registrar of voters, election commission, or county board of elections) and ask what you can do. People who are concerned with improving the election process could become poll workers. Today this job often requires some background with computers; consequently, counties are seeking younger poll workers. (Some cities like Philadelphia have laws preventing an individual from serving as a poll

> "People who want to improve the elections could become poll workers. As Election Day approaches, political parties and campaigns also need volunteers to watch polling places, contact voters, give elderly or ailing voters rides, and much more."

worker in consecutive elections, which exacerbates a shortage of qualified help.[146]) County offices typically hire temporary workers several months before Election Day to help with processing registrations and absentee ballots. They may also need people to coordinate with voter registration drives or help with vote counts on Election Day.[147]

And then there are many things to do if you want to work with political parties, candidates, or activist groups. Political parties and campaign need volunteers to staff the polls, contact voters, and provide infirm voters with rides to polls. Election advocates, from those running voter hotlines to the League of Women Voters to local election integrity activists, also need help on Election Day. Some monitor problems reported by voters. Some track exit poll results. All you have to do is call and ask.

STATE-BY-STATE VOTING GUIDE

DETAILED INFORMATION ON VOTING IN YOUR STATE

Author's note: The information that follows has been compiled from websites of secretaries of state or statewide election boards from all 50 states and the District of Columbia, the National Conference of State Legislatures (www.ncsl.org), VotersUnite.org's Election Problem log (2004 to present), www.electionline.org, www.verifiedvoting.org/verifier/, www.votetrustusa.org, and www.advancementproject.org.

It is intended to provide voter registration requirements and deadlines, voter ID requirements, names of officials to contact, and information on voting systems used, and it highlights issues that have been problems in recent elections. In states offering early voting, or in-person voting before Election Day, those deadlines are noted. Users should always check with local election officials to verify the information and be aware of any new changes in law or practices.

ALABAMA

TO REGISTER TO VOTE, YOU MUST:

- Be a U.S. citizen
- Reside in Alabama
- Be at least 18 years old
- Not have been convicted of a felony punishable by imprisonment in the penitentiary (or, you must have had your civil and political rights restored)
- Not currently be declared mentally incompetent
- Swear or affirm to "support and defend the Constitution of the U.S. and the State of Alabama and further disavow any belief or affiliation with any group which advocates the overthrow of the governments of the U.S. or the State of Alabama by unlawful means and that the information contained herein is true, so help me God."

Registration Deadline: Voter registration is closed 10 days before an election. Applications must be postmarked or delivered by the 11th day prior to the election (Friday, Oct. 24, 2008).

Secretary of State Website: www.sos.state.al.us/elections/voterregistrationinfo.aspx

OFFICIALS TO CONTACT

The secretary of state election website has voter registration information and forms that can be downloaded or requested by mail.. The site also allows people to request a form by mail and has links to county boards of registrars, where people can also register. The site also has contact information for county election officials.

People can also register at motor vehicle departments and various state social agencies and some libraries.

VOTER ID REQUIREMENTS

ID is required of all voters, but the state accepts a wide range of ID cards including government photo IDs, utility bills, bank statement, paycheck, military ID, and hunting, gun, and fishing licenses. Voters without ID can cast a provisional ballot; if two poll workers identify them, they can cast a standard vote.

VOTING MACHINES

Alabama uses paper ballots that are counted by optical scanners. Voters with disabilities use ballot-marking devices.

ELECTION CONCERNS

The state has a history of computer voting malfunctions dating to the 2002 gubernatorial election. More recently, it has had difficulties with creating a new statewide voter database before the primaries. Voters should verify that their registration information is correct. During the 2008 primary, some precincts did not open on time, and others lacked voting machines.

EARLY VOTING

Not permitted before Election Day, but qualified voters can get an absentee ballot to vote by mail. It must be received the day before the election.

ALASKA

TO REGISTER TO VOTE, YOU MUST:

- Be a U.S. citizen
- Be at least 18 years old within 90 days of this registration
- Not be a convicted felon (unless unconditionally discharged)
- Not be judicially determined to be of unsound mind, unless the disability has been removed
- Not be registered to vote in another state

Registration Deadline: 30 days before the election (Sunday, Oct. 5, 2008; last day to be postmarked is Saturday, Oct. 4)

VOTER ID REQUIREMENTS

Before being allowed to vote, each voter must show one form of ID: a voter registration card, driver's license, birth certificate, passport, hunting or fishing license, current utility bill, pay stub or government document with the voter's name and address.

Poll workers can waive the ID requirement if they know the voter. A voter without ID can cast a provisional ballot.

VOTING MACHINES

Alaska uses a paper ballot optical-scan system. Voters with disabilities use direct-recording electronic (DRE) machines with voter-verified paper trail printers.

OFFICIALS TO CONTACT

The state Division of Elections oversees Alaska elections. Voter registration applications are available online and can be turned in, mailed or faxed to regional offices in Anchorage, Juneau, Nome, Fairbanks, and Wasilla. The website also has information on polling places, where to vote, absentee voting, and other details.

State Election Website:
www.elections.state.ak.us/

Lt. Governor Website:
http://ltgov.state.ak.us/

EARLY VOTING

Anyone eligible to vote may vote early in person 15 days before an election. The locations of absentee voting offices are listed by community at:
www.ltgov.state.ak.us/elections/avo.htm

ARIZONA

TO REGISTER TO VOTE, YOU MUST:

- Be a U.S. citizen
- Be a resident of Arizona and your county at least 29 days preceding the next election
- Be 18 years old on or before the next general election
- Not have been convicted of treason or a felony (or, you must have had your civil rights restored)
- Not currently be declared an incapacitated person by a court of law
- Provide proof of citizenship

Registration Deadline: 29 days before the election (Monday, Oct. 6, 2008).

OFFICIALS TO CONTACT

Arizonans can register to vote by visiting the secretary of state website, which is bilingual. There is an online registration option; the form can also be printed and mailed to a county recorder's office. A list of those offices also is available online.

State Election Website:
www.azsos.gov/election/

Secretary of State Website:
www.azsos.gov/

VOTER ID REQUIREMENTS

ID is required of all voters. Photo ID is not mandatory. Those without ID are issued a provisional ballot and must present ID within five days of the election. Arizona is also the first state to require that newly registered voters provide proof of citizenship.

VOTING MACHINES

Arizona uses paper ballot optical-scan systems. Voters with disabilities use direct-recording electronic (DRE) machines with a voter-verified paper trail or ballot-marking devices.

ELECTION CONCERNS

During the 2008 primary, registration problems led to more than 10,000 people receiving provisional ballots because their names were not on voter rolls. Voters need to verify that their registration information is current and correct.

EARLY VOTING

Early voting begins Oct. 2, 2008.

ARKANSAS

TO REGISTER TO VOTE, YOU MUST:

- Be a U.S. citizen
- Be an Arkansas resident at least 31 days before the election
- Live at the address in Box 2 of your voter application
- Be at least 18 years old on or before the next election
- Not be a convicted felon (or, you must have had your sentence completely discharged or have been pardoned)
- Not be presently adjudged as mentally incompetent
- Not claim the right to vote in any other jurisdiction

Registration Deadline: 30 days before the election (Monday, Oct. 6, 2008)

OFFICIALS TO CONTACT

Arkansas residents can register to vote at county clerk's offices and state revenue, driver services, public assistance, and military recruitment offices, as well as public libraries. Voters are only considered registered after they have received an acknowledgment from their county clerk, but the secretary of state website allows voters to verify their registration online.

State Election Website:
www.sosweb.state.ar.us/elections.html

Secretary of State Website:
www.sosweb.state.ar.us/

VOTER ID REQUIREMENTS

ID is required of all voters, but photo ID is not mandatory. Those without ID may cast provisional ballots.

VOTING MACHINES

The state uses paper ballot optical-scan systems and direct-recording electronic (DRE) machines, both with and without a voter-verified paper trail.

ELECTION CONCERNS

Electronic voting machines experienced a range of breakdowns in the primary, from not starting up to printer malfunctions, to vote counts that were doubled, to machines recording a choice other than the candidate selected by the voter. People should verify that their vote and/or the printout of their vote is accurate.

EARLY VOTING

Early voting starts Oct. 20.

CALIFORNIA

TO REGISTER TO VOTE, YOU MUST:

- Be a U.S. citizen
- Be a resident of California
- Be at least 18 years of age at the time of the next election
- Not be imprisoned or on parole for the conviction or a felony
- Not currently be judged mentally incompetent by a court of law

Registration Deadline: 15 days before the election (Monday, Oct. 20, 2008)

OFFICIALS TO CONTACT

The secretary of state's website has bilingual registration information. You can request a voter registration form online, which will be mailed to you, but you will not be registered to vote until your county elections office receives a signed copy of this form. You can also pick up a form at your county elections office, library, or U.S. post office.

State Election Website: www.ss.ca.gov/elections/elections.htm
Secretary of State Website: www.ss.ca.gov/

VOTER ID REQUIREMENTS

ID is required of all voters. Photo and non-photo ID are accepted, including a state driver's license, passport, employee ID card, credit or debit card, military ID, student ID card, health club ID card, insurance plan ID card, sample ballot, voter notification card, public housing ID card, lease or rental agreement and any government document with the voter's name and address.

VOTING MACHINES

The secretary of state decertified most paperless voting machines and then recertified them with conditions. All but two counties use voter-marked paper ballots as the primary voting system. Voters with disabilities use direct-recording electronic (DRE) systems with a voter-verified paper trail or ballot-marking devices.

ELECTION CONCERNS

During the primary, some counties ran out of paper ballots due to high turnout. In a few counties there also were some ballot design errors that slowed the count or confused voters. These problems delayed voters and slowed the counting of ballots.

EARLY VOTING

Early voting begins 29 days before Election Day.

COLORADO

TO REGISTER TO VOTE, YOU MUST:

- Be a U.S. citizen
- Be a resident of Colorado 30 days prior to election
- Be 18 years old on or before Election Day
- Not be confined as a prisoner or serving any part of a sentence under mandate

Registration Deadline: 29 days before the election. If the application is received in the mail without a postmark, it must be received within five days of the close of registration (Monday, Oct. 6, 2008).

OFFICIALS TO CONTACT
The secretary of state website has lists and links to the county clerk and recorders, which process voter registration forms and can verify registration information and polling place location. The site also allows voters to verify their registration information online.

State Election Website: www.elections.colorado.gov/DDefault.aspx?/main.htm

Secretary of State Website: www.sos.state.co.us/

VOTER ID REQUIREMENTS
ID is required of all voters, but photo ID is not mandatory. Accepted ID includes state driver's license or revenue card, government photo ID, pilot's license, military ID, current utility bill, or naturalization document.

VOTING MACHINES
Voting machines have been controversial in Colorado. In 2006, electronic poll books crashed, notably in Denver. In response, the secretary of state sought to replace direct-recording electronic (DRE) systems with paper ballot optical-scan systems. Many local officials protested early in 2008, and the secretary relented. Voters will use either voter-marked paper ballots or DREs with a voter-verified paper trail.

ELECTION CONCERNS
Voters should verify their registrations are correct and bring the required ID in case electronic voter list trouble recurs. Voters should also be careful when marking paper ballots with pens to avoid optical-scan counters misreading their votes.

EARLY VOTING
Early voting starts 10 days before the election.

CONNECTICUT

TO REGISTER TO VOTE, YOU MUST:

- Be a U.S. citizen
- Be a resident of Connecticut and of the town in which you vote
- Be 18 years old on or before the next election
- Not be convicted of a felony, except conviction for nonsupport (or, you must have had your civil rights restored)

Registration Deadline: Voters may register in person until noon on the last business day before an election (Tuesday, Oct. 21, 2008).

OFFICIALS TO CONTACT

The secretary of state's website has voter registration forms and registration information in English and Spanish. The website also has a "Find Your Elected Officials" directory including registrars of voters and town clerks, the local officials who maintain voter lists.

State Election Website:
http://www.sots.ct.gov/sots/cwp/browse.asp?A=3179

Secretary of State Website:
www.sots.ct.gov/

VOTER ID REQUIREMENTS

ID is required of all voters, but photo ID is not mandatory. Social Security cards and other forms of printed identification showing the voter's name, address, signature, or photograph are accepted. Voters also can sign a state form attesting to their identity.

VOTING MACHINES

The state uses paper ballot optical-scan systems and a vote-by-phone system for voters with disabilities.

ELECTION CONCERNS

Some towns ran out of ballots in the primary, and there were a few instances of optical-scan voting machines malfunctioning.

EARLY VOTING

Early voting by mail is only permitted to a small number of qualified voters, such as members of the military — not the general public.

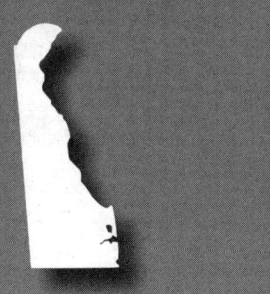

DELAWARE

TO REGISTER TO VOTE, YOU MUST:

- Be a U.S. citizen
- Be a permanent resident of Delaware
- Be at least 18 years old on the date of the next general election
- Not be a convicted felon
- Not be mentally incompetent

Registration Deadline: 20 days prior to the general election and 20 days prior to any primary election (Saturday, Oct. 11, 2008)

OFFICIALS TO CONTACT

The commissioner of elections oversees elections in Delaware. Registration forms are available online, as are maps to find your polling place and a tracking system to follow the progress of verifying a provisional ballot.

State Election Website:
www.elections.delaware.gov/

Questions can be answered by sending an e-mail to COE_VOTE@State.de.us

VOTER ID REQUIREMENTS

The state's ID requirements are flexible. First-time voters must submit a copy of a current and valid photo ID or a copy of a current utility bill, bank statement, paycheck, government check, or other government document that shows your name and address. If an established voter does not have ID with them at the polls, they can sign an affidavit attesting to their identity.

VOTING MACHINES

The state uses direct-recording electronic (DRE) systems without a voter-verified paper record.

ELECTION CONCERNS

There were some problems with voting machines during the 2008 primary, so voters should speak to poll workers if there are any difficulties or malfunctions as the DREs have no paper trail.

EARLY VOTING

Early voting by mail is only permitted to a small number of qualified voters, such as members of the military — not the general public.

DISTRICT OF COLUMBIA

TO REGISTER TO VOTE, YOU MUST:

- Be a U.S. citizen
- Be a resident of the District of Columbia at least 30 days preceding the next election
- Be at least 18 years old on or preceding the next election
- Not be in jail for a felony conviction
- Not have been judged "mentally incompetent" by a court of law
- Not claim the right to vote anywhere outside D.C.

Registration Deadline: 30 days before the election (Monday, Oct. 6, 2008)

OFFICIALS TO CONTACT

The district's Board of Elections and Ethics oversees voting. Its website has online registration forms and information such as checking and changing registration information, finding polling places, using voting machines, and requesting absentee ballots.

State Election Website: www.dcboee.org/

VOTER ID REQUIREMENTS

The district's ID requirements are flexible. It accepts a valid and current photo ID, utility bill, paycheck, or any other government document with the voter's name and address on it.

VOTING MACHINES

Voters in the District are given the option of using a paper ballot optical-scan voting system or direct-recording electronic (DRE) machines without voter-verified paper trail printers.

ELECTION CONCERNS

During the primary, many polling places ran out of paper ballots, delaying voters. Also, some voting machines broke down, causing ballots to be put in piles for later counting.

EARLY VOTING

A voter may cast an in-person absentee ballot at the Board of Elections and Ethics Office Monday through Saturday beginning 15 days before the election and ending the day before the election.

FLORIDA

TO REGISTER TO VOTE, YOU MUST:

- Be a U.S. citizen
- Be a legal resident of Florida and the county in which you seek to be registered
- Be 18 years old (you may preregister if you are 17)
- Not currently be adjudicated mentally incapacitated with respect to voting in Florida or any other state

Registration Deadline: 29 days before the election (Monday, Oct. 6, 2008)

State Election Website: http://election.dos.state.fl.us/

Secretary of State Website: www.dos.state.fl.us/

OFFICIALS TO CONTACT
The state's Division of Elections oversees elections and voter registration. The website has bilingual voter registration forms, which must be submitted to the county office of any supervisor of elections (or to the elections division), any motor vehicle department, any voter registration agency, or any armed forces recruitment office.

VOTER ID REQUIREMENTS
Only photo ID is accepted. Acceptable forms are a Florida driver's license or state ID card issued by the motor vehicle department, other government ID, credit/debit cards, employee badges, retirement center IDs, etc. The card must have a signature on it. Voters without correct ID must cast provisional ballots.

VOTING MACHINES
In May 2007, Republican Gov. Charlie Crist signed a bill requiring all counties to use voter-marked paper ballots as the primary voting system. Most voters with disabilities will use direct-recording electronic (DRE) machines without voter-verified paper trail printers, while some will use ballot-marking devices.

ELECTION CONCERNS
Florida voters, especially those with unusually spelled or hyphenated names, must check their voter registration information to ensure it is current and accurate. Under state law, correcting any mistakes is the responsibility of the voter, not the government. The state has a history of making registration errors, and there is ongoing litigation surrounding the state's voter lists.

EARLY VOTING
The early voting period is 15 to 2 days prior to the election. A voter must present a photo and signature ID. Each supervisor of elections will designate the times and places for early voting in his or her county 30 days before the election.

GEORGIA

TO REGISTER TO VOTE, YOU MUST:

- Be a U.S. citizen
- Be a legal resident of Georgia and the county in which you want to vote
- Be 18 years old within six months after the day of registration, and be 18 years old by Election Day
- Not be serving a sentence for a felony
- Not have been judicially determined to be mentally incompetent, unless the disability has been removed

Registration Deadline: Deadline is the fifth Monday before any primary, general election, or presidential preference primary, or regularly scheduled special election (Monday, Oct. 6, 2008).

State Election Website:
www.sos.state.ga.us/elections/default.htm

SOS Website:
www.sos.state.ga.us/default800.asp

OFFICIALS TO CONTACT

The Georgia secretary of state oversees elections. The office's website has links to print a voter registration form and to contact your county registrar of voters, as well as absentee and early voting information. Registration forms can be returned to the secretary of state or county registrars.

VOTER ID REQUIREMENTS

All voters must present a photo ID.

VOTING MACHINES

The state uses direct-recording electronic (DRE) machines without a voter-verified paper record.

ELECTION CONCERNS

Many election integrity advocates are concerned that Georgia's new voter ID law could disenfranchise people who lack photo IDs or the paperwork necessary to obtain the ID. However, in the primary the big problem in some counties was a shortage of electronic poll book computers to check in voters. Verify your ID is correct, and expect lines.

EARLY VOTING

One week before Election Day (from Oct. 27 to Oct. 31, 2008). The state elections division announces voting locations.

HAWAII

TO REGISTER TO VOTE, YOU MUST:

- Be a U.S. citizen
- Be a resident of Hawaii
- Be at least 16 years old (you must be 18 years old by Election Day in order to vote)
- Not be in jail for a felony conviction
- Not be "non compos mentis"

Registration Deadline: 30 days before the election (Monday, Oct. 6, 2008)

State Election Website: www.hawaii.gov/elections

Voter Registration Website: http://hawaii.gov/elections/voters/registration.htm

OFFICIALS TO CONTACT
The Hawaii Office of Elections oversees elections in concert with city and county clerks. Its website has voter registration forms, absentee voting forms and information, and maps with polling place locations.

VOTER ID REQUIREMENTS
Hawaii requires voters to have a photo ID with a signature to verify identity. Voters are asked to sign poll books to record that the voter voted at the polling place. A voter registration notice is not accepted as ID.

VOTING MACHINES
Hawaii uses paper ballot optical-scan systems and direct-recording electronic (DRE) systems with a voter-verified paper audit trail.

ELECTION CONCERNS
Hawaii is the midst of transitioning to new voting systems. A high-turnout election could see lines at the polls if there is trouble with the new machines.

EARLY VOTING
You may vote by absentee ballot in person at the office of your city or county clerk. Call for exact dates and times.

IDAHO

TO REGISTER TO VOTE, YOU MUST:

- Be a U.S. citizen
- Be a resident of and in the county for 30 days prior to the day of election
- Be at least 18 years old
- Not have been convicted of a felony, without having been restored to the rights of citizenship, or not be confined in prison on conviction of a criminal offense

Registration Deadline: You may register at polls on Election Day.

State Election Website: http://www.idahovotes.gov/

Secretary of State Website: www.idsos.state.id.us/

OFFICIALS TO CONTACT

Voter registration in Idaho is at the county level, with the county clerk acting as the chief registration official of their respective county. The idahovotes.gov website has registration forms, absentee voting, and other information.

VOTER ID

You may register at the polls on Election Day by providing proof of residence. All proof-of-residence documents must be accompanied by a photo ID. For ID, the state accepts current and valid photo IDs, student IDs, and any document with a current address. First-time voters who register by mail must show ID before voting.

VOTING MACHINES

The state uses a mix of systems: paper ballot optical-scan systems, punch cards, hand-counted paper ballots, with ballot-marking devices for voters with disabilities.

EARLY VOTING

Any qualified voter may vote early in person at an absentee polling place. The dates, times, and places of absentee polling places are available from the voter's local county clerk. In-person absentee voting ends at 5 p.m. the day before an election.

ILLINOIS

TO REGISTER TO VOTE, YOU MUST:

- Be a U.S. citizen
- Be a resident of Illinois and of your election precinct at least 30 days before the next election
- Be at least 18 years old on or before the next election
- Not be in jail for a felony conviction
- Not claim the right to vote anywhere else

Registration Deadline: 28 days prior to each election (Tuesday, Oct. 7, 2008)

State Election Website:
www.elections.state.il.us/

Secretary of State Website:
http://www.cyberdriveillinois.com//

OFFICIALS TO CONTACT
The Illinois State Board of Elections, county clerks, and local election commissioners oversee elections. The state board of election website provides registration materials as well as the names and contact information for local election officials.

VOTER REQUIREMENTS
A current and valid photo ID, or a copy of a current utility bill, bank statement, government check, paycheck, or any government document with the name and address of the voter is accepted. First-time voters who register by mail must present ID before voting.

VOTING MACHINES
Illinois uses a mix of paper ballot optical-scan systems, direct-recording electronic (DRE) machines with voter-verified paper trails, and ballot-marking devices for voters with disabilities.

ELECTION CONCERNS
There were a variety of voting machine breakdowns during the 2008 primary in the Chicago area, including machines that did not properly label the candidates or count ballots. Some poll workers were confused, in one case giving pens with no ink to voters and saying they would be read by scanners.

EARLY VOTING
Twenty-two to five days before an election (Oct. 14 through Oct. 30). Early voting polling places and times are listed by local jurisdiction.

INDIANA

TO REGISTER TO VOTE, YOU MUST:

- Be a U.S. citizen
- Be a resident in the precinct at least 30 days before the next election
- Be at least 18 years of age on the day of the next general election
- Not currently be in jail for a criminal conviction

Registration Deadline: 29 days before the election (Monday, Oct. 6, 2008)

State Election Website:
www.in.gov/sos/elections/

Voter Information Portal:
http://www.in.gov/sos/elections/voters/index.html

VOTER ID REQUIREMENTS

Indiana has the country's toughest voter ID law. A photo ID must meet these criteria to be acceptable for voting: display the voter's name and match the registration record; be current or have expired since the last general election; and be issued by the state of Indiana or federal government. Not all student IDs from Indiana universities meet these criteria. Those without proper ID can cast provisional ballots, but they must return within 10 days to present further proof to their county election board.

VOTING MACHINES

The state uses a mix of paper ballot optical-scan systems and direct-recording electronic (DRE) systems without voter-verified paper ballot trails.

OFFICIALS TO CONTACT

The election division in the secretary of state's office and the county election boards oversee voting in Indiana. The secretary of state's website has voter registration information, forms, and an online search to check voter registration and polling place location. The online registration search page also has contacts for county officials.

ELECTION CONCERNS

Indiana's voter ID law has disenfranchised people who have not brought the proper ID to the polls. Additionally, the state's new voter center — which consolidated polling places in rural areas — has been confusing for both poll workers and voters, causing delays in voting. There also were some DRE breakdowns. Voters should ensure they have the proper ID and anticipate long lines.

EARLY VOTING

Some counties allow early voting at designated sites 15 days before an election. Early voting dates, times, and places are available from the voter's local county election board office.

IOWA

TO REGISTER TO VOTE, YOU MUST:

- Be a U.S. citizen
- Be a resident of Iowa
- Be at least 17 1/2 years old (you must be 18 to vote)
- Not have been convicted of a felony (or, you must have had your rights restored)
- Not currently be judged "mentally incompetent" by a court
- Give up the right to vote in any other place

Registration Deadline: As of January 2008, Iowa allows you to register to vote on Election Day at the polling place for the precinct you currently live in. If you register to vote on Election Day, you will be required to show proof of residence and an ID. For voters registering before Election Day, the deadline is 10 days before the general election and 11 days before all other elections.

State Election Website: www.sos.state.ia.us/

Secretary of State Website: www.sos.state.ia.us/

VOTER ID REQUIREMENTS

A current and valid photo ID or current utility bill, bank statement, government check, paycheck, or other government document with the name and address of the voter are accepted. All first-time voters must show ID before voting. If you do not have proof of residence, another voter in your precinct may attest to your identity and address. All other voters receive provisional ballots.

VOTING MACHINES

In April, the governor signed a bill authorizing the state to complete a transition to a paper ballot optical-scan system for the November 2008 elections. Voters with disabilities use ballot-marking devices.

ELECTION CONCERNS

There have been some problems with optical-scan equipment malfunctioning during the tabulation phase in recent elections. Voters could face some delays if turnout is high and poll workers are using new voting systems for the first time.

OFFICIALS TO CONTACT

The secretary of state's website has voter registration forms and related information for Election Day registration and absentee voting. All forms must be turned in to your county auditor. The secretary of state website also has links and contact information for these offices.

EARLY VOTING

You may vote at your county auditor's office prior to any election. You cannot take the ballot home with you. The county auditor's office is open on the two Saturdays directly before all primary and general elections. On Election Day, you may not vote by absentee ballot at the auditor's office.

KANSAS

TO REGISTER TO VOTE, YOU MUST:

- Be a citizen of the United States
- Be a resident of Kansas
- Be 18 by the next statewide general election
- Not be imprisoned for conviction in any state or federal court of a crime punishable by death or imprisonment for one year or longer (or, you must have had your civil rights restored)
- Not claim the right to vote in any other location or under any other name
- Not be excluded from voting for mental incompetence by a court of competent jurisdiction

Registration Deadline: Registration must be delivered by mail 15 days before the election (Monday, Oct. 20, 2008).

State Election Website:
www.kssos.org/elections/elections.html

Secretary of State Website:
www.kssos.org/

VOTER ID REQUIREMENTS
Photo and non-photo ID is accepted, including a current Kansas driver's license, non-driver state ID card, utility bill, bank statement, paycheck or paycheck stub, or government document showing the voter's name and address.

VOTING MACHINES
The state uses a mix of paper ballot optical-scan systems, direct-recording electronic (DRE) systems with and without a voter-verified paper trail, ballot-marking devices and hand-counted paper ballots.

ELECTION CONCERNS
Kansas has created vote centers in several counties, consolidating precincts. Voters need to know where those centers are and be sure to turn in their ballots at the proper precinct.

OFFICIALS TO CONTACT
Kansas elections are conducted by the counties with oversight by the secretary of state's office. Voter registration application forms must be submitted to the county election officer where the applicant lives. The secretary of state website has registration forms and instructions in English and Spanish, maps of election districts and lists of registered voters.

EARLY VOTING
Advance voting begins Wednesday, Oct. 15, 2008, and continues through noon Monday, Nov. 3, 2008, in person at county election offices. Advance voting ballots must be received by the close of polls on Nov. 4, 2008. Exact dates and times for early voting may vary by county.

KENTUCKY

TO REGISTER TO VOTE, YOU MUST:

- Be a U.S. citizen
- Be a resident of Kentucky
- Be a resident of the county for at least 28 days prior to the election date
- Be 18 years of age on or before the next general election
- Not be a convicted felon (or, if you have been convicted of a felony, your civil rights must have been restored by executive pardon)
- Not have been judged "mentally incompetent" in a court of law
- Not claim the right to vote anywhere outside of Kentucky

Registration Deadline: 29 days before the election (Monday, Oct. 6, 2008)

State Election Website:
www.sos.ky.gov/elections/

Voter Registration Website:
http://elect.ky.gov/register.htm

VOTER ID REQUIREMENTS
Photo and non-photo ID is accepted from voters, including a state driver's license, social security card, or a credit card.

VOTING MACHINES
Kentucky mostly uses direct-recording electronic (DRE) systems without voter-verified paper trails. Seven counties, including the largest, Jefferson County, use paper ballot optical-scan systems.

EARLY VOTING
Early in-person voting is available at the local county clerk's office between Oct. 17 and Nov. 3 for the general election for some voters, such as those who are traveling or in the military, precinct officers, or pregnant women.

OFFICIALS TO CONTACT
The State Board of Elections administers the commonwealth's election laws, supervises voter registration, appoints political party representatives to the 120 county boards of elections, and certifies the official election results. The board of election's website has registration forms and instructions. It also has a "Voter Information Center" where people can check their registration and contact information for county clerks.

LOUISIANA

TO REGISTER TO VOTE, YOU MUST:

- Be a U.S. citizen
- Reside in the state and parish in which you seek to register and vote
- Be at least 17 years old, and be 18 years old prior to the next election to vote
- Not currently be under an order of imprisonment for conviction of a felony
- Not currently be under a judgment of full interdiction or limited interdiction where your right to vote has been suspended

Registration Deadline: 30 days before the election (Monday, Oct. 6, 2008)

State Election Website:
http://www.sos.louisiana.gov/tabid/68/Default.aspx

Secretary of State Website:
www.sec.state.la.us/

OFFICIALS TO CONTACT

The secretary of state and parish registrar of voters' offices oversee elections. Voter registration forms are available online and at parish registrar offices and can be returned to both locations. The state's motor vehicle department, social service agencies, offices serving people with disabilities, and military recruitment offices also are voter registration agencies. The secretary of state website also has a directory of parish election officials and polling place information.

VOTER ID REQUIREMENTS

A photo ID is requested of all voters. Those without a state driver's license, state special ID card, or generally recognized picture ID can bring a utility bill, payroll check or government document with their name and address on it. Those without a photo ID must sign an affidavit before voting.

VOTING MACHINES

The state uses direct-recording electronic (DRE) systems without a voter-verified audit trail.

ELECTION CONCERNS

Since Hurricanes Katrina and Rita, many displaced residents have not been able to vote. Critics have faulted the state for not setting up satellite voting centers. During the 2008 primary, hundreds of Louisiana Democrats went to the polls only to find they were listed as Independent or unaffiliated voters on voter rolls. In June, Republicans complained Democratic boter registration efforts were creating "phony" applications. Voters should verify their registration information and correct errors.

EARLY VOTING

Early voting is conducted at the parish registrar of voters office. The early voting period is from 12 to 6 days before the election (Oct. 21 to Oct. 28, 2008). The hours are 8:30 a.m. to 4:30 p.m.

MAINE

TO REGISTER TO VOTE, YOU MUST:

- Be a U.S. citizen
- Be a resident of Maine and the municipality in which you want to vote
- Be at least 17 years old (you must be 18 to vote)
- Not be under guardianship because of mental illness

Registration Deadline: You can register to vote until, and including, Election Day. There is no cutoff date for registering to vote in person at your town office or city hall.

State Election Website:
www.maine.gov/sos/cec/elec/

Voter Information Website: http://maine.gov/sos/cec/elec/voter_info/index.html

OFFICIALS TO CONTACT
Maine's elections are supervised by the secretary of state but administered by municipal clerks or registrars. The secretary of state website has voter registration forms, contact information for local officials, polling place locations, and links to civic participation groups.

VOTER ID REQUIREMENTS
Maine driver's license or other valid photo ID, a current utility bill, bank statement, paycheck, or government document that shows the voter's name and address.

VOTING MACHINES
Maine uses voter marked paper ballots statewide counted by hand or by optical scanners with a vote-by-phone system available in each polling place for voters with disabilities.

ELECTION CONCERNS
Maine was one of 16 states recently sued or pressured by the Department of Justice to purge voter rolls. That came after the state had trouble with a private vendor updating voter rolls. People should bring ID to vote in case they were mistakenly purged. The state has Election Day registration to ensure that everyone can vote.

EARLY VOTING
Registered voters may vote early in person at their local municipal clerk's office 30 to 45 days before the election, as soon as absentee ballots are available. No application is required.

MARYLAND

TO REGISTER TO VOTE, YOU MUST:

- Be a U.S. citizen
- Be a resident of Maryland and the county in which you want to vote
- Be at least 18 years old before the next general election
- Not be under sentence, or on probation or parole following conviction for an infamous crime (that is, any felony, treason, perjury, or any crime involving an element of deceit, fraud, or corruption)
- Not have been convicted more than once of an infamous crime, without a pardon
- Not be under guardianship for mental disability

Registration Deadline: 9 p.m. 21 days before the election (Tuesday, Oct. 14, 2008)

State Election Website:
www.elections.state.md.us/

Registration Information Website:
http://www.elections.state.md.us/voter_registration/index.html

OFFICIALS TO CONTACT

Voting in Maryland is overseen by the state board of elections and run by county and city boards of election. The state election website has voter registration forms and contact information for local election officials. Voters must contact the local election board to verify registration information.

VOTER ID REQUIREMENTS

First-time voters must have a Maryland driver's license, state ID card or Social Security card for their registration to be processed. To vote, a current or valid photo ID, copy of a current utility bill, bank statement, or government document with the voter's name and address is required.

VOTING MACHINES

Maryland's governor signed a law for the state to transition to optically scanned paper ballots by 2010, but for the 2008 general election the state will be using direct-recording electronic (DRE) systems without voter-verified paper trails.

ELECTION CONCERNS

During the 2008 primary, problems were reported with voters' names omitted from electronic poll books (although this was a bigger problem in 2006) and DRE voting machines not starting or operating properly. A state study group in May called for more voting machines, a voter hotline, and better communication between state and local election officials. The state BOE said people who want to avoid lines in November should vote absentee or vote during off-hours. Voter should verify their registration, bring correct ID, and have patience.

EARLY VOTING

It is not permitted in this state to vote in person before Election Day, but voters can get an absentee ballot application and vote early by mail.

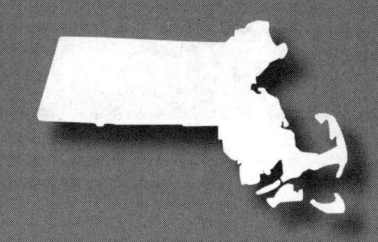

MASSACHUSETTS

TO REGISTER TO VOTE, YOU MUST:

- Be a U.S. citizen
- Be a resident of Massachusetts
- Be 18 years old
- Not have been convicted of corrupt practices in respect to elections
- Not be under guardianship with respect to voting

Registration Deadline: 20 days before the election (Wednesday, Oct. 15, 2008)

State Election Website:
http://www.sec.state.ma.us/ele/

Secretary of the Commonwealth Website:
www.sec.state.ma.us/

OFFICIALS TO CONTACT
The secretary of the commonwealth oversees elections in Massachusetts in concert with town or city election offices. The secretary's website has voter registration forms and information. Under "My Election Information," voters can verify their registration. Another link demonstrates voting machines. People can register by mail or at local election offices, or state motor vehicle offices. Town or city clerks have polling place information.

VOTER ID REQUIREMENTS
Acceptable ID must include your name and address where you are registered to vote, such as a current state driver's license, photo ID, current utility bill, bank statement, paycheck, or government document. First-time voters must present ID to vote.

VOTING MACHINES
Massachusetts uses paper ballots statewide, counted either with optical-scanners or by hand. Voters with disabilities use a ballot-marking device.

ELECTION CONCERNS
The state was one of 16 pressured to purge voter rolls by the Justice Department in early 2007. Voters should verify that their registration information is valid.

EARLY VOTING
Voters who will be away on Election Day or are unable to go to the polls due to a disability or religious belief can vote absentee at their local clerk or election commission office. They should contact that office three weeks before the election.

MICHIGAN

TO REGISTER TO VOTE, YOU MUST:

- Be a U.S. citizen
- Be a resident of Michigan and the city or township where you are applying to register to vote
- Be 18 years old by the next election
- Not be confined in a prison after having been convicted and sentenced

Registration Deadline: 30 days before the election (Monday, Oct. 6, 2008)

Secretary of State Website:
www.michigan.gov/sos

State Election Website:
http://www.michigan.gov/sos/0,1607,7-127-1633-49313--,00.html

OFFICIALS TO CONTACT

The secretary of state and local city or township clerk's office oversee elections in Michigan. Voter registration information and forms are available at the "Michigan Voter Information Center" on the secretary's website. The site also has a tool to verify voter registrations. Completed registration forms are submitted to local clerk offices.

VOTER ID REQUIREMENTS

All Michigan voters must show a photo ID or sign an affidavit attesting that he or she is not in possession of a photo ID.

VOTING MACHINES

Michigan uses paper ballot optical-scan systems statewide. Voters with disabilities use ballot-marking devices.

ELECTION CONCERNS

In 2004, Republican volunteers challenged the credentials of some inner-city voters, causing tension and delays at some polls. There was also some confusion in 2006 among voters who did not bring photo IDs. Voters should bring the proper photo IDs to vote, immediately solving any challenge or need to sign an affidavit.

EARLY VOTING

Early voting is not permitted in this state, but qualified voters can vote absentee by mail.

MINNESOTA

TO REGISTER TO VOTE, YOU MUST:

- Be a U.S. citizen
- Be a resident of Minnesota for 20 days before the next election
- Be 18 years old by Election Day
- Not be convicted of treason or a felony (or, you must have had your civil rights restored)
- Not be under guardianship or found legally incompetent

Registration Deadline: Election Day registration. You also may register to vote by mail or in person at your county courthouse (at least 20 days before the election to appear on the roster, which is Tuesday, Oct. 14, 2008) or at your polling place on Election Day.

Secretary of State Website:
www.sos.state.mn.us/home/index.asp

State Election Center: http://www.sos.state.mn.us/home/index.asp?page=204

OFFICIALS TO CONTACT

Minnesota's secretary of state and county election officials oversee elections. Registration applications can be submitted by mail or in person at county courthouses. The secretary of state website has a directory of these locations, registration forms (in English and five other languages), a polling place finder tool, and other information.

VOTER ID REQUIREMENTS

The state accepts many forms of ID including a driver's license or state ID card, a current student ID, a current student fee statement with valid address in combination with another photo ID, a Native American tribal ID card or government document with the voter's name, street address, and signature. Voters without a photo ID can have another voter from the same precinct attest to their identity.

VOTING MACHINES

Minnesota uses paper ballot optical-scan systems statewide. Voters with disabilities use ballot-marking devices.

EARLY VOTING

A registered voter may vote early in person if he or she will be away from home on Election Day, is ill or disabled, will be serving as an election judge in a precinct not his own, or will be unable to go to the polls due to a religious observance. The voter may vote at his county auditor or city or township clerk's office in the 30 days before Election Day.

MISSISSIPPI

TO REGISTER TO VOTE, YOU MUST:

- Be a U.S. citizen
- Have lived in Mississippi and in your county (and city, if applicable) 30 days before the election in which you want to vote
- Be 18 years old by the time of the general election in which you want to vote
- Have not been convicted of murder, rape, bribery, theft, arson, obtaining money or goods under false pretense, perjury, forgery, embezzlement, or bigamy (or, you must have had your rights restored as required by law)
- Not have been declared mentally incompetent by a court

Registration Deadline: 30 days before the election (Monday, Oct. 14, 2008)

State Election Website: www.sos.state.ms.us/elections/voterinfoguide.asp

Voter Registration Website: http://www.sos.state.ms.us/elections/VoterRegistration/index.asp

VOTER ID REQUIREMENTS

Photo and non-photo ID is accepted, including a state driver's license, paycheck, utility bill, or other government document that includes a name and address.

VOTING MACHINES

The state mostly uses direct-recording electronic (DRE) voting machines with a voter-verified paper trail, although a few counties use DREs without a paper trail and others use paper ballot-based optical-scan systems.

ELECTION CONCERNS

Toughening the state's voter ID law has been a big partisan fight in 2008. Voters should be sure to bring the proper ID so there are no complications. There also have been difficulties with operating DRE voting machines in recent elections, from poll worker confusion to the paper trail not printing. Voters should verify their votes.

OFFICIALS TO CONTACT

The Mississippi secretary of state and county voter registrars oversee the state's elections. The secretary of state's election division website has an online registration application and contact information for the county registrars. County clerks need to receive applications at least 30 days before an election.

EARLY VOTING

Registered voters may vote early in person if they will be outside their county of residence on Election Day or are disabled, ill, over 65 years of age, or in the military, or for other specified reasons. Eligible voters may vote early in person at the circuit clerk's office no later than noon Nov. 1 for the general election.

MISSOURI

TO REGISTER TO VOTE, YOU MUST:

- Be a U.S. citizen
- Be a resident of Missouri
- Be at least 17 1/2 years of age (you must be 18 to vote)
- Not be on probation or parole after conviction of a felony
- Not be convicted of a felony or misdemeanor connected with the right of suffrage
- Not be declared incompetent by any court of law
- Not be confined under a sentence of imprisonment

Registration Deadline: 5 p.m. on the fourth Wednesday prior to the election (Wednesday, Oct. 8, 2008)

State Election Website:
www.sos.mo.gov/elections/

Voter Information Website:
www.sos.mo.gov/elections/s_default.asp?id=voters

OFFICIALS TO CONTACT

The elections division of the office of the secretary of state is responsible for administering all statewide elections in concert with county clerks. The election division website has voter registration forms, contacts for county clerks (where registrations are to be submitted), polling place locations, and other information. Voters can also register at motor vehicle and state social agencies.

VOTER ID REQUIREMENTS

ID is required of all voters, but non-photo IDs are accepted. Acceptable forms include any government ID, college ID, utility bill, bank statement, or paycheck with the name and address of the voter. If you do not possess any of these IDs, you may still cast a ballot if two supervising election judges, one from each major political party, attest they know you.

VOTING MACHINES

Missouri uses a paper ballot optical-scan system. Voters with disabilities use direct-recording electronic (DRE) systems equipped with voter-verified paper trail printers.

ELECTION CONCERNS

Enacting tougher voter ID laws was a bitter partisan fight in Missouri in 2008, although proposals for stricter ID laws failed to pass the Legislature. Still, voters — particularly in the core of the state's biggest cities — should bring proper ID and anticipate the possibility of challenges to their voter credentials at their voting place, as that tactic has been used in previous presidential elections by supporters of stronger voter ID laws.

EARLY VOTING

A registered voter may vote early in person at the office of his local election official from six weeks before the election until the day before the election.

MONTANA

TO REGISTER TO VOTE, YOU MUST:

- Be a U.S. citizen
- Be a resident of Montana and of the county in which you want to vote for at least 30 days before the next election
- Be at least 18 years of age on or before the election
- Not be in a penal institution for a felony conviction
- Not currently be determined by a court to be of unsound mind
- Meet these qualifications by the next election day if you do not currently meet them

Registration Deadline: 30 days before the election (Monday, Oct. 6, 2008), or Election Day at the county election office.

State Election Website: www.sos.mt.gov/ELB/Voter_Information.asp

SOS Website: www.sos.mt.gov/

OFFICIALS TO CONTACT

The secretary of state and local election administrators oversee voting in Montana. The secretary of state's website has registration applications and a directory of local election officials, who prefer to receive the application 30 days before the election. However, these officials will accept applications until the close of polls on Election Day except between noon and 5 p.m. on the day before an election. Polling place location and other information is on the site.

VOTER ID REQUIREMENTS

All voters must show ID, but photo and non-photo ID is accepted. Any current ID with a voter's name and current address, such as driver's license, school ID, current utility bill, bank statement, paycheck, voter confirmation notice, or government document is acceptable.

VOTING MACHINES

Montana uses paper ballots that are counted either by hand or by optical-scan computers. Voters with disabilities use ballot-marking devices.

EARLY VOTING

Any registered voter may vote early in person starting 30 days before Election Day. Voters must go to their local election office, apply for an absentee ballot and then vote. Call local election offices for exact dates, times and places for early voting.

NEBRASKA

TO REGISTER TO VOTE, YOU MUST:

- Be a U.S. citizen
- Be a resident of Nebraska
- Be at least 18 years of age or be 18 on or before the first Tuesday after the first Monday of November
- Not have been convicted of a felony (or, if convicted, you must have had your civil rights restored)
- Not have been officially found to be mentally incompetent

Registration Deadline: Mail-in voter registrations must be postmarked on or before the third Friday preceding an election. Individuals may register in person at the county clerk/election commissioner's office prior to 6 p.m. on the second Friday preceding an election (Friday, Oct. 24, or mail by Friday, Oct, 17, 2008).

State Election Website:
www.sos.ne.gov/elec/2008/index.html

Secretary of State Website:
www.sos.state.ne.us/

VOTER ID REQUIREMENTS
ID is required, but any current photo and non-photo ID is accepted, as is a utility bill, bank statement, paycheck, or government document with the name and address of the voter.

VOTING MACHINES
The state uses paper ballots that are either counted by optical-scan systems or by hand. Voters with disabilities use ballot-marking devices.

EARLY VOTING
All registered voters can complete an early voting application allowing them to cast their ballot at any county election office 35 days before an election.

OFFICIALS TO CONTACT
The secretary of state, county clerks and election commissioners oversee voting in Nebraska. The secretary of state's website has registration forms, contacts for county clerks, polling place information, and other voting information. County election officials will contact voters by mail to confirm that the application is correct and accepted.

NEVADA

TO REGISTER TO VOTE, YOU MUST:

- Be a U.S. citizen
- Have attained the age of 18 years on the date of the next election
- Have continuously resided in Nevada, in your county, at least 30 days and in your precinct at least 10 days before the next election
- Not currently be laboring under any felony conviction or other loss of civil rights that would make it unlawful for you to vote
- Not be determined by a court of law to be mentally incompetent
- Claim no other place as your legal residence

Registration Deadline: Deadline is Oct. 4, 2008, if you register to vote by mail and Oct. 14, 2008, if you register to vote in person.

State Election Website: www.sos.state.nv.us/elections/

OFFICIALS TO CONTACT

The secretary of state, county clerks and voter registrars oversee voting. Registration forms are available at the secretary of state website, as is contact information for county election officials (the forms can be turned in at their offices). Other information, such as voters' rights and absentee voting, is also online.

VOTER ID REQUIREMENTS

All voters must show ID, such as a current and valid photo ID, or a copy of a current utility bill, bank statement, paycheck, or government document with the name and address of the voter.

VOTING MACHINES

Nevada uses direct-recording electronic (DRE) systems with a voter-verified paper trail. Voters with disabilities use ballot-marking devices.

ELECTION CONCERNS

New voters should verify that their registrations are properly processed, as some groups conducting voter registration drives in 2004 did not submit forms from people who registered with one party.

EARLY VOTING

Registered voters may vote early in person between Oct. 18 and Oct. 31, 2008, for the general election at their county clerk's office or at temporary polling places to be established by the county clerk. Call for those locations.

NEW HAMPSHIRE

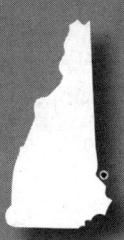

TO REGISTER TO VOTE, YOU MUST:

- Be a U.S. citizen
- Be at least 18 years of age
- Have a permanent established domicile in New Hampshire
- Not have been denied the right to vote by reason of a felony conviction

Registration Deadline: New Hampshire has Election Day registration. You can register at your polling place. New Hampshire town and city clerks accept absentee voter forms 10 days before the election.

State Election Website:
http://www.sos.nh.gov/electionsnew.htm

Secretary of State Website:
www.sos.nh.gov/index.html

OFFICIALS TO CONTACT

The secretary of state and town or city clerks oversee voting. Voter registration forms are available at the local clerks' offices. There is no required residence period before being allowed to vote. The secretary of state website has contacts for municipal clerks.

VOTER ID REQUIREMENTS

Photo and non-photo ID is required. The state accepts current and valid photo IDs as well as a current utility bill, bank statement, paycheck, or government document with a name and address.

VOTING MACHINES

New Hampshire uses paper ballots in small towns and paper ballots that are optically scanned and tabulated in larger communities. Voters with disabilities use a vote-by-phone system available in each polling place.

EARLY VOTING

New Hampshire does not have early in-person voting, but voters who will be away can apply for an absentee ballot.

NEW JERSEY

TO REGISTER TO VOTE, YOU MUST:

- Be a U.S. citizen
- Be a resident of New Jersey and at your address at least 30 days before the next election
- Be at least 18 years of age by the time of the next election
- Not be serving a sentence or on parole or probation as the result of a conviction of any indictable offense under the laws of this or another state or of the United States

Registration Deadline: 21 days before the election (Tuesday, Oct. 14, 2008)

State Election Website:
http://www.njelections.org/

Secretary of State Website:
www.state.nj.us/state/

OFFICIALS TO CONTACT

New Jersey's division of election, county commissioners of registration and municipal clerks oversee voting. The division of election website has voter registration applications, which are to be mailed to the registration commissioner's office in the voter's county. People can also register to vote in person at most state and county social agencies, as well as at military recruiting offices. The election website also has a polling place locator tool.

VOTER ID REQUIREMENTS

ID is required, but many forms of photo and non-photo ID are accepted. These include current driver's license, student or job ID, military or government ID, or passport. Also acceptable are bank statements, car registration, government documents, rent receipts, a sample ballot, or a utility bill with the voter's name and address.

VOTING MACHINES

New Jersey uses direct-recording electronic (DRE) voting machines without a voter-verified paper trail.

ELECTION CONCERNS

During the primary, several counties experienced problems with electronic vote counts. In one county, the statewide voter database scrambled the political parties of registrants. New Jersey also has been pushed by the Justice Department to purge voter rolls. Voters should verify that their voter registrations are accurate and speak to poll workers if their DREs are not operating properly.

EARLY VOTING

New Jersey does not permit in-person early voting. Voters can apply for an absentee ballot from their county clerk, which must be mailed by Oct. 28, 2008.

NEW MEXICO

TO REGISTER TO VOTE, YOU MUST:

- Be a U.S. citizen
- Be a resident of New Mexico
- Be at least 18 years of age at the time of the next election
- Not have been denied the right to vote by a court of law by reason of mental incapacity or felony conviction

Registration Deadline: 28 days before the election (Tuesday, Oct. 7, 2008)

Secretary of State Website: www.sos.state.nm.us/

OFFICIALS TO CONTACT

The secretary of state oversees elections, but county clerks register voters and run the elections. The secretary of state's "frequently asked questions" page has links to verify voter registration, registration forms, overseas ballot information, and county clerk telephones and addresses The Secretary of State Bureau of Elections can answer questions and direct you to your county clerk.

VOTER ID REQUIREMENTS

ID is required of all voters, but the state accepts a wide range of ID cards including government photo IDs, utility bills, student IDs, and bank statements. The state also allows voters to make a verbal statement, which is unusual. Voters without ID can cast provisional ballots.

VOTING MACHINES

New Mexico uses paper ballots that are counted by optical scanners. Voters with disabilities use ballot-marking devices.

ELECTION CONCERNS

Established voters need to verify that their registration information is current and correct. During the 2008 Democratic presidential caucus, voter rolls had accuracy problems. As a result, 17,000 people received a provisional ballot. Counties were using a new statewide voter database, with names omitted or listed under an incorrect political party.

EARLY VOTING

Registered voters can cast ballots 28 days before the election until the Saturday preceding Election Day.

NEW YORK

TO REGISTER TO VOTE, YOU MUST:

- Be a U.S. citizen
- Be a resident of the county, or of the city of New York, at least 30 days before an election
- Be 18 years old by the date of the general, primary, or other election in which your want to vote
- Not be in jail or on parole for a felony conviction
- Not currently be judged incompetent by order of a court of competent judicial authority
- Not claim the right to vote elsewhere

Registration Deadline: 25 days before the election (Friday, Oct. 10, 2008)

State Board of Election Website: www.elections.state.ny.us

http://www.elections.state.ny.us/voting.html

VOTER ID REQUIREMENTS
ID is required, but photo and non-photo ID is accepted. Photo IDs can include driver's license, military ID, employee ID, student ID, and government-issued IDs. Acceptable non-photo ID includes utility bills, paychecks, or government documents with the voter's name and address.

VOTING MACHINES
New York State will be using mechanical-lever voting machines in November 2008. Voters with disabilities use ballot-marking devices.

ELECTION CONCERNS
The big question was whether the state would be moving to new voting systems to be used for the first time in the presidential election; this is not the case.

OFFICIALS TO CONTACT
The state and county election boards oversee voting. The state board of elections website has registration forms, a directory of county boards of elections (where people can register in person), and a list of more than a dozen state agencies where voters also may register. Voters also can verify their registrations online.

EARLY VOTING
A registered voter may vote early in person at his county board of elections office if he will be unavoidably absent from his county on Election Day. The voter may vote no earlier than 30 days before the election and no later than the day before the election. The voter must fill out an absentee ballot application.

NORTH CAROLINA

TO REGISTER TO VOTE, YOU MUST:

- Be a U.S. citizen
- Be a resident of North Carolina and the county in which you live for at least 30 days prior to the election
- Be 18 years of age by the day of the next general election
- Have your rights of citizenship restored if you have been convicted of a felony
- Not be registered to vote in any other county or state

Registration Deadline: 25 days before the election (Friday, Oct. 10, 2008)

State Election Website:
www.sboe.state.nc.us/

http://www.sboe.state.nc.us/content.aspx?id=23

OFFICIALS TO CONTACT

The state and county boards of elections oversee voting. The state board of elections website has a main registration page with links to voter registration forms, individual voter information, polling places, local election official contacts, and other useful information. Voters can also register at the department of motor vehicles and a variety of state social service agencies. The state also has a new program allowing people to register and vote by absentee ballot 19 to 3 days before an election. Ask the county board of elections for locations.

VOTER ID REQUIREMENTS

ID is required, but a current photo and non-photo ID is accepted. The state also accepts current utility bills, bank statement, paychecks, and government documents with the name and address of the voter.

VOTING MACHINES

North Carolina uses a mix of paper ballot optical-scan systems and direct-recording electronic (DRE) systems with a voter-verified paper trail. Voters with disabilities use ballot-marking devices.

ELECTION CONCERNS

There were reports from the 2008 primary that voters' names had been scrambled in one county's database. A new advocacy group seeking to register women also sent out confusing registration information and made possibly illegal phone calls. New voters should verify their registrations. There also were reports from several counties that optical scanners had double-counted ballots, although election officials corrected the errors.

EARLY VOTING

Any eligible voter may register and vote early in person with "One Stop Early Voting." Early voting is conducted between 19 days and 3 days before the election at times and locations determined by the local county boards of elections.

NORTH DAKOTA

North Dakota is the only state that does not have voter registration. However, to vote in North Dakota you must be:

- A U.S. citizen
- At least 18 years old on the day of an election
- A legal North Dakota resident
- A resident in the precinct for 30 days preceding the election

For the purposes of voting, a person may have only one residence.

State Election Website:
www.nd.gov/sos/

http://www.nd.gov/sos/electvote/voting/index.html

OFFICIALS TO CONTACT
Elections are overseen by the secretary of state and county election officials, who are primarily county auditors. The secretary of state website has a list of these officials, early and absentee ballot information, early voting locations, and information for college and military voters.

VOTER ID REQUIREMENTS
ID is required, but photo and non-photo ID is accepted, including a driver's license, state ID card, any government-issue ID, tribal ID, student ID, military ID, utility bill dated 30 days prior to Election Day with the name and address, and U.S. Postal Service change-of-address notice. Poll workers can also vouch for the identity of a voter, or the voter can sign an affidavit at the polls.

VOTING MACHINES
North Dakota uses paper ballot optical-scan voting systems. Voters with disabilities use ballot-marking devices.

EARLY VOTING
Some counties, during the 15 days prior to an election, open an early voting precinct so that voters of the county can stop by and vote whenever they happen to be near the voting location. Check with local officials for places and hours.

OHIO

TO REGISTER TO VOTE, YOU MUST:

- Be a U.S. citizen
- Be a resident of Ohio for at least 30 days before an election
- Be 18 years old on or before Election Day. If you will be 18 on or before the day of the general election, you may vote in the primary election for candidates only.
- Not be convicted of a felony and currently incarcerated
- Not be found incompetent by a court for purposes of voting
- Not have been permanently disenfranchised for violations of the election laws

Registration Deadline: 30 days before the election (Monday, Oct. 6, 2008)

State Election Website:
www.sos.state.oh.us/

http://www.sos.state.oh.us/SOS/voter.aspx

OFFICIALS TO CONTACT

The secretary of state and county boards of election oversee voting. The secretary of state's website has registration forms and a directory of county election boards, where the forms are to be submitted. It also has a polling place locater tool and information about absentee voting.

VOTER ID REQUIREMENTS

All voters are required to show ID, but photo and non-photo IDs are accepted, including driver's license, military IDs, a current utility bill, bank statement, paycheck, or government document that shows the voter's name and address.

VOTING MACHINES

In early 2008, the secretary of state ordered the state's most populous county to use a paper ballot optical-scan system for the primary. Ohio uses a mix of paper ballot optical-scan systems and direct-recording electronic (DRE) systems with a voter-verified paper trail. Voters with disabilities use ballot-marking devices.

ELECTION CONCERNS

During the primary, some voters who asked for paper ballots as an alternative to using direct-recording electronic (DRE) machines were mistakenly given provisional ballots, not regular ballots. In some counties, DREs did not list all the candidates or ballot issues and also had trouble tabulating votes. Voters should verify registration information, as voters were purged as late as August 2004 in some counties.

EARLY VOTING

Any registered voter may vote early in person at his county board of elections office after absentee ballots are available, usually 35 days before Election Day. The last day for in-person absentee voting is the day before the election.

OKLAHOMA

TO REGISTER TO VOTE, YOU MUST:

- Be a U.S. citizen and Oklahoma resident
- Be 18 years old on or before the date of the next election
- Have not been convicted of a felony, for which a period of time equal to the original sentence has not expired, or for which you have not been pardoned
- Not now be under judgment as an incapacitated person or a partially incapacitated person prohibited from registering to vote

Registration Deadline: 25 days before the election (Friday, Oct. 10, 2008)

State Election Website:
www.oklaosf.state.ok.us/~elections/

Secretary of State Website:
www.sos.state.ok.us/

OFFICIALS TO CONTACT

The state election board and county election boards oversee voting. Registration forms are available online, as is a directory of county election boards. The county boards approve the application and send voters identification cards listing their name, address, political affiliation, and polling place. Bring the card when voting.

VOTER ID REQUIREMENTS

ID is required, but photo and non-photo ID is accepted, including a current driver's license or other photo ID or a utility bill, paycheck, bank statement, or government document that shows the voter's name and address.

VOTING MACHINES

Oklahoma uses paper ballot optical-scan voting systems. Voters with disabilities use a vote-by-phone system available in each polling place.

EARLY VOTING

Any registered voter may vote early in person on the Friday or Monday before an election; if a state or federal office is on the ballot, people may also vote from 8 a.m. to 1 p.m. on the Saturday before the election. The voter should contact his county election board for details.

OREGON

TO REGISTER TO VOTE, YOU MUST:

- Be a U.S. citizen
- Be a resident of Oregon
- Be at least 18 years old by Election Day

Registration Deadline: 21 days before the election (Tuesday, Oct. 14, 2008)

In 1998 voters passed a ballot measure directing that all elections be conducted by mail. Instead of using traditional polling places where voters go to cast ballots on Election Day, a ballot is mailed to each registered voter. The ballot is then returned to the county elections office and is counted on Election Day.

State Election Website:
www.oregonvotes.org

Secretary of State Website:
www.sos.state.or.us/

OFFICIALS TO CONTACT

The secretary of state's election division and county election offices oversee voting. Registration by mail is now the method most people use. Forms are available at the secretary of state and county websites, in most banks and public buildings, and in many state agencies. These websites have other information on voting deadlines.

VOTER ID REQUIREMENTS

Voters must provide a current, valid ID to register. Accepted forms include an Oregon driver's license or state ID. If the voter lacks these, they must provide the last four digits of their Social Security number. If the individual does not have these, they must affirm this and provide a copy of a valid photo ID, paycheck stub, utility bill, bank statement, or government document with their name and address.

VOTING MACHINES

Paper ballot voting systems — all vote by mail. Voters with disabilities use ballot-marking devices in county election offices if they vote in person on Election Day.

ELECTION CONCERNS

An advocacy group seeking to register female voters sent out confusing letters early in 2008, causing some voters to question whether their registrations were valid; in many cases, they were. In 2004, a GOP-connected voter registration firm did not submit voter registrations from Democrats. Voters should verify their registration by contacting their county elections office.

EARLY VOTING

All registered voters are sent a ballot 14 to 18 days before the election. The ballot contains instructions for voting at home and returning the ballot. Voters who do not receive their ballots two weeks before the election should contact their county office.

PENNSYLVANIA

TO REGISTER TO VOTE, YOU MUST:

- Be a U.S. citizen at least one month before the next election
- Be a resident of Pennsylvania and your election district at least 30 days before the election
- Be at least 18 years of age on the day of the next election
- Not have been confined in a penal institution for the conviction of a felony within the past five years

Registration Deadline: 30 days before an election or primary (Monday, Oct. 6, 2008)

State Election Website: http://www.votespa.com/

Secretary of State Website: www.dos.state.pa.us/dos/site/default.asp

OFFICIALS TO CONTACT

The Pennsylvania Department of State and county election and voter registration officials oversee elections. The department's online voter information and resource center, www.votespa.com, has multilingual (eight languages) registration forms, information for voters in varying situations (college student to senior to ex-felons), contacts for county election officials, a polling place locator tool, and voting system demonstrations.

VOTER ID REQUIREMENTS

ID is required of all voters, but photo and non-photo ID is accepted. Acceptable photo ID includes a driver's license, any government ID, student ID, employee ID, or passport. Acceptable non-photo IDs include any state or federal ID, firearm permit, current utility bill, current bank statement, or paycheck.

VOTING MACHINES

Most of the state votes on direct-recording electronic (DRE) systems with no voter-verified paper trail. Several counties use paper ballot optical-scan systems, with DREs or ballot-marking devices for voters with disabilities.

ELECTION CONCERNS

During the 2008 primary, there were many reports of DRE voting machines malfunctioning at the start of voting, causing voters to leave. Voters also told election hotlines that their party registrations were incorrectly listed on voter rolls. Voters should anticipate potential delays and verify their registration information.

EARLY VOTING

Early in-person voting is not permitted in Pennsylvania, but a registered voter may vote early by mail if they meet one of several qualifications such as traveling on Election Day, serving in the military, or being disabled.

RHODE ISLAND

TO REGISTER TO VOTE, YOU MUST:

- Be a U.S. citizen
- Be a resident of Rhode Island for 30 days preceding the next election
- Be 18 years old by Election Day
- Be neither serving a sentence, including probation or parole, upon final conviction of a felony imposed on any date; nor serving any sentence, whether incarcerated or suspended, on probation or parole, upon final conviction of a felony committed after Nov. 5, 1986
- Not have been lawfully judged to be mentally incompetent

Registration Deadline: 30 days before the election (Saturday, Oct. 4, 2008)

State Election Website: www.sec.state.ri.us/elections

http://www.elections.state.ri.us/registration/intro.htm

VOTER ID REQUIREMENTS
ID is required. First-time voters must present a driver's license or the last four digits of their Social Security number. Other forms of acceptable ID are a current photo ID or copy of a current utility bill, bank statement, government check, paycheck, or government document with the voter's name and address.

VOTING MACHINES
Rhode Island uses paper ballot optical-scan voting systems. Voters with disabilities use ballot-marking devices.

ELECTION CONCERNS
During the 2008 primary, there were reports of voters who said their political party was incorrectly stated on voter lists. Voters should verify their registration information.

OFFICIALS TO CONTACT
The Rhode Island Board of Elections and local boards of canvassers oversee voting. The state board of elections website has voter registration forms, which are to be sent to the local election officials for processing. The site also has information on voting absentee, polling places, and a thorough "Frequently Asked questions" page. Voters can also register in person at the division of motor vehicles and many state social service agencies.

EARLY VOTING
It is not permitted in this state, but registered voters may vote early by mail if they meet one of several qualifications, such as being absent from the state or too ill or mentally or physically disabled to vote on Election Day, or having religious tenets that would prevent them from voting. The board of canvassers must receive absentee ballot applications at least 21 days before the election.

SOUTH CAROLINA

TO REGISTER TO VOTE, YOU MUST:

- Be a U.S. citizen
- Be a resident of South Carolina
- Be at least 18 years old on or before the next election
- Not be confined in any public prison as a result of a conviction of a crime
- Never have been convicted of a felony or offense against election laws (or, if previously convicted, you must have served your entire sentence, including probation or parole; or, you must have received a pardon for the conviction)
- Not be under a court order declaring you mentally incompetent
- Claim the address on the application as your only legal place of residence and claim no other place as your legal residence

Registration Deadline: 30 days before the election (Monday, Oct. 20, 2008)

State Election Website:
http://www.scvotes.org/

http://www.scvotes.org/south_carolina_voter_registration_information

VOTER ID REQUIREMENTS

ID is required. To vote, you must present a voter registration certificate, valid South Carolina driver's license, or a photo ID issued by the South Carolina Department of Motor Vehicles.

VOTING MACHINES

South Carolina uses direct-recording electronic (DRE) systems without a voter-verified paper trail.

ELECTION CONCERNS

Voters in the 2008 Republican primary in Horry County experienced widespread delays when DREs malfunctioned upon open and close of voting. Local election officials struggled to fix the machines and provide paper ballots. While the problems did not appear in the subsequent Democratic primary, voters should give themselves enough time to vote should the problem recur.

OFFICIALS TO CONTACT

The South Carolina election commission and county boards of voter registration oversee elections. Registration applications are available at the state election commission website, as well as at the county registration board offices. The state website has contacts for county officials as well as online tools to check and update your registration information. Check with local officials for your polling place.

EARLY VOTING

Voters may apply for an absentee ballot and vote the same day at a local voter registration office if they meet one of the qualifications, such as being a student, in the military, physically disabled, over 65 years of age, or unable to vote on Election Day due to employment. The last day to apply for an absentee ballot in person and vote is the day before the election. Contact the county office for details.

SOUTH DAKOTA

TO REGISTER TO VOTE, YOU MUST:

- Be a U.S. citizen
- Reside in South Dakota
- Be 18 years old by the next election
- Not be under a sentence of imprisonment for a felony conviction
- Not have been adjudged mentally incompetent by a court

Registration Deadline: Registration must be received 15 days before the election (Monday, Oct. 20, 2008)

State Election Website:
www.sdsos.gov/electionsvoteregistration/
electionsVoteregistration_overview.shtm

OFFICIALS TO CONTACT

The secretary of state and county auditors oversee elections. The secretary of state's website has registration forms and a directory of county auditors, where the forms are to be sent. People can also register in person at motor vehicle departments, county auditor offices, state human service agencies, and military recruitment offices. New voters will be contacted by their county auditor within 15 days and told their application has been received.

VOTER ID REQUIREMENTS

ID is required of all voters, with the state requesting photo IDs. If a voter does not have a photo ID, they may sign an affidavit and then cast a ballot. Acceptable forms of ID include a state driver's license or photo ID card, any government or tribal photo ID, or student photo ID.

VOTING MACHINES

South Dakota uses paper ballot optical-scan voting systems. Voters with disabilities use ballot-marking devices.

ELECTION CONCERNS

In the 2004 presidential election, partisan poll workers intimidated some Native American voters and voter registration groups did not submit all completed forms to county officials. Voters should use the secretary of state website "Voter Information Portal" to verify registration information and bring the proper ID to vote.

EARLY VOTING

Registered voters may vote early in person from Sept. 23 until Election Day at their local county auditor's office.

TENNESSEE

TO REGISTER TO VOTE, YOU MUST:

- Be a U.S. citizen
- Be a resident of Tennessee
- Be at least 18 years old on or before the next election
- Not have been convicted of a felony, or if convicted, have had your full rights of citizenship restored (or have received a pardon)
- Not be adjudicated incompetent by a court of competent jurisdiction (or have been restored to legal capacity)

Registration Deadline: 30 days before the election (Monday, Oct. 6, 2008)

State Election Website: http://state.tn.us/sos/election/

OFFICIALS TO CONTACT

The Department of State's Division of Elections and county election commissions oversee voting. The election division website has registration forms and contacts for the county commissions, where the forms are to be submitted. The website also has pages on voting by mail, overseas voting, early voting, restoration of voting rights, voter ID, and voting machines. People can also register in person at county election offices, the state motor vehicles division, various social service agencies, and public libraries.

VOTER ID REQUIREMENTS

ID is required, but photo and non-photo ID is accepted. Voters can present a current voter registration card, state driver's license, or a photo ID with their name and address. If they do not have any of these, they can present another photo ID, utility bill, bank statement, paycheck, or government document with their name and address, as well as any document with their name and signature. Voters can also sign an affidavit of identity at their polling place.

VOTING MACHINES

The Legislature recently passed a bill requiring any new voting systems purchased after Jan. 1, 2009 be paper-based. However, for 2008, most voters will use direct-recording electronic (DRE) systems without a voter-verified paper trail. Two counties use mixed paper ballot systems and DREs without the paper trail.

EARLY VOTING

Any registered voter may vote between Oct. 15 and Oct. 30, 2008. Voters should contact their county election commission for early voting locations and times.

TEXAS

TO REGISTER TO VOTE, YOU MUST:

- Be a U.S. citizen
- Be a resident of the county in which the application for registration is made
- Be at least 17 years and 10 months old (you must be 18 to vote)
- Not be convicted of a felony. (However, felons regain the right to register when pardoned, two years after receiving a certificate of discharge from the appropriate correction institution, or two years after completing a period of probation.)
- Have not been declared mentally incompetent by final judgment of a court of law

Registration Deadline: 30 days before the election (Monday, Oct. 6, 2008)

State Election Website:
www.sos.state.tx.us/elections/index.shtml

OFFICIALS TO CONTACT

The secretary of state and county registrars and clerks oversee voting. The secretary of state website has an "Election and Voting Information" page with registration forms and contacts for local election officials, who can validate registrations and change registration information, and who know the early voting options. Once registered, voters will receive a "registration certificate," which must be presented when voting.

VOTER ID REQUIREMENTS

All voters must present registration certificates. Those without these documents can present a state driver's license, a photo ID, a birth certificate, citizenship papers, a passport, an official government mailing to that voter, or a copy of a current utility bill, bank statement, paycheck, or any government document with their name and address.

VOTING MACHINES

Texas uses a mix of paper ballot voting systems and direct-recording electronic (DRE) machines without voter-verified paper trails. Voters with disabilities use ballot-marking devices.

ELECTION CONCERNS

Some legislators are reviving talk of imposing a stricter voter ID law. The state also has been pressured by the U.S. Department of Justice to purge its voter rolls. How these trends will unfold before the 2008 election is unclear, but voters should check their registration status and bring the proper ID to the polls to avoid problems. In May, the state settled a suit in which it pledged to stop prosecuting campaign volunteers in minority communities who help seniors vote by mail but who forget to sign their names to the ballot envelope.

EARLY VOTING

Any registered voter may vote early in person between Oct. 20 and Oct. 31, 2008. The voter should contact his early voting clerk for information on places and times for early voting.

UTAH

TO REGISTER TO VOTE, YOU MUST:

- Be a U.S. citizen
- Be a resident in Utah for 30 days immediately before the next election
- Be at least 18 years old on or before the next election
- Not be convicted of treason or a crime against the elective franchise, unless restored to civil rights
- Not be found to be mentally incompetent by a court of law

Registration Deadline: Registration forms sent in the mail to county clerks must be postmarked 30 days before the election. Voters can also register in person at county clerk offices up to 15 days before an election (Oct. 20, 2008), but those voters will not be eligible to vote early.

State Election Website:
www.elections.utah.gov/

http://www.elections.utah.gov/voterinformation.html

VOTER ID REQUIREMENTS
ID is required, but photo and non-photo ID is accepted, including a state driver's license, state ID card, passport, current utility bill, or government document that shows the voter's name and address.

VOTING MACHINES
Utah uses direct-recording electronic (DRE) systems equipped with voter-verified paper trail printers.

ELECTION CONCERNS
During the 2008 primary, voters in one county experienced problems with new electronic poll books, resulting in long lines and causing people to leave without voting. The state also has been pressured by the U.S. Department of Justice to purge its voter lists. Voters should verify their registrations and give themselves enough time to vote.

OFFICIALS TO CONTACT
The state's elections office and county clerks oversee elections. The state's website has voter registration forms and contacts for county clerks, where the forms are to be submitted. Voters who move or change their name or party affiliation must re-register.

EARLY VOTING
Any registered voter may vote early in person between Oct. 21 and Oct. 31, 2008. The voter should contact his local county clerk for details on times and locations of early polling places.

VERMONT

TO REGISTER TO VOTE, YOU MUST:

- Be a U.S. citizen
- Be a resident of Vermont
- Be 18 years of age on or before Election Day

Registration Deadline: Applications must be delivered to the town clerk before 5 p.m. on the Wednesday preceding the day of the election (Wednesday, Oct. 29, 2008).

State Election Website:
http://vermont-elections.org/elections1/voters.html

OFFICIALS TO CONTACT
The secretary of state and municipal clerks and registrars oversee voting. The secretary of state website has registration forms, a directory of town and city clerks and registrars, tools to locate polling places and see the voting system used, options for voters with disabilities, and other information. New registrants submit forms to local officials who administer an oath or ask people to sign an affirmation before voting.

VOTER ID REQUIREMENTS
ID is required, but photo and non-photo ID is accepted, including a valid photo ID, copy of a current utility bill, bank statement, government check, paycheck, or any government document with the voter's name and address.

VOTING MACHINES
Vermont uses paper ballot voting systems, some that are counted by hand or tabulated by optical scanners. Voters with disabilities use a vote-by-phone system available in each polling place.

VOTING ISSUES
Vermont was among the states pressured by the U.S. Department of Justice to purge its voter rolls, so voters should verify their registrations with local voting officials.

EARLY VOTING
Registered voters may vote early in person at their local town clerk's office from 30 days before an election until the day before an election.

VIRGINIA

TO REGISTER TO VOTE, YOU MUST:

- Be a U.S. citizen
- Be a resident of Virginia and of the precinct in which you want to vote
- Be 18 years old by the next election
- Not have been convicted of a felony (or, you must have had your civil rights restored)
- Not currently be declared mentally incompetent by a court of law

Registration Deadline: Applications must be delivered 29 days before the election (Monday, Oct. 6, 2008).

State Election Website: http://www.sbe.virginia.gov/cms/Voter_Information/Index.html

OFFICIALS TO CONTACT

The state board of election and local electoral boards and general registrars oversee voting. The state board of elections website has forms and instructions to register, and tools to find and contact local registration offices, vote absentee and check absentee status, find polling places, and other information. People also can register at motor vehicle department offices, state social agencies, public libraries, and military recruitment offices. You must provide your Social Security number, if any, when registering in Virginia.

VOTER ID REQUIREMENTS

Voters must provide ID or sign an "affirmation of identification" at the polls to vote. Virginia accepts photo and non-photo ID, including a state voter ID card, valid state driver's license, military ID, government-issue ID, employee ID, or Social Security card. Voters can also present a current utility bill, bank statement, government check or paycheck, or government document with their name and address.

VOTING MACHINES

Most of the state votes on direct-recording electronic (DRE) systems without a voter-verified paper trail; however, a few of the most populous counties use a mix of paper ballot systems and DREs without voter-verified paper trails. Three counties use all paper ballot voting systems.

ELECTION CONCERNS

During the 2008 primary, there were reports of long lines and shortages of poll workers to check in voters in various parts of the state. There also were some problems with DREs. In one county, two-thirds of their machines did not work properly at the start of voting, and blind voters reported that an audio component mangled one presidential candidate's name. Voters should give themselves enough time to vote in November.

EARLY VOTING

Registered voters may vote early in person if they qualify for absentee voting. Early in-person voting usually begins 45 days before the election and ends three days before the election. Voters must first complete an application at their local registrar's office and can vote in that same visit.

WASHINGTON

TO REGISTER TO VOTE, YOU MUST:

- Be a U.S. citizen
- Be a legal resident of Washington State, your county, and your precinct for 30 days immediately preceding the election in which you want to vote
- Be at least 18 years old by Election Day
- Not be convicted of an infamous crime (or, you must have your civil rights restored)
- Not be judicially declared mentally incompetent

Registration Deadline: 30 days before the election, or delivered in person to the local voter registration office 15 days before the election (Monday, Oct. 4, 2008, or Monday, Oct. 20 in person).

State Election Website:
www.secstate.wa.gov/elections/

http://www.secstate.wa.gov/elections/auditors.aspx

VOTER ID REQUIREMENTS

The entire state votes by mail with the exception of King and Pierce counties. Those voting at the polls must provide ID. Acceptable forms include a driver's license, state ID card, student ID card, tribal ID card, voter registration card, current utility bill, bank statement, paycheck, or government document with the voter's name and address. A voter who does not have ID may cast a provisional ballot.

VOTING MACHINES

While most of the state votes by mail, all county election offices have voting systems for people with disabilities. These systems are ballot-marking devices that produce completed ballots, or direct-recording electronic (DRE) systems with voter-verified paper trails. In King and Pierce counties, voters use a mix of paper ballot systems and DREs with a paper trail.

OFFICIALS TO CONTACT

Elections are administered by the secretary of state and at the local level by county auditors (except King County, which has the Records, Elections and Licensing Services Division). These offices assist with registering to vote, requesting an absentee ballot, and other election-related services. The secretary of state's website has voter registration forms (in 11 languages) and an interactive map with contact information for local election officials.

EARLY VOTING

Washington state does not have early in-person voting, but any registered voter may vote early by mail. An absentee ballot may be requested from the voter's county auditor's office by phone, mail, fax, electronically, or in person. Absentee ballots are available 20 days before each election.

WEST VIRGINIA

TO REGISTER TO VOTE, YOU MUST:

- Be a U.S. citizen
- Live in West Virginia
- Be 18 years old or, to vote in the primary, be 17 years old and turning 18 before the general election
- Not be under conviction, probation, or parole for a felony, treason, or election bribery
- Not have been judged "mentally incompetent" in a court of competent jurisdiction

Registration Deadline: 20 days before the election (Wednesday, Oct. 15, 2008)

State Election Website:
www.wvsos.com/elections/candidates/electionpages.htm#Voting

OFFICIALS TO CONTACT

The secretary of state and county clerks oversee voting. Registration forms are available on the secretary of state website and can be mailed to county clerks. (The website has contact information for the clerks.) If voters do not receive a notice in the mail within two to three weeks, they should contact their county clerk. The website also has pages for absentee voting, a voter help line, descriptions of voting machines, and other information. People also can register at the county clerk's office at their county courthouse, motor vehicle departments, state social service agencies, and military recruiting offices.

VOTER ID REQUIREMENTS

ID is required, but photo and non-photo ID is accepted. Forms of acceptable ID include a driver's license, pay stubs, bank statements, utility bills, or government-issued documents with the voter's name and address.

VOTING MACHINES

The state uses a mix of paper ballot voting systems and direct-recording electronic (DRE) systems with voter-verified paper trails. Voters with disabilities use ballot-marking devices.

ELECTION CONCERNS

During the primary season, a new advocacy group seeking to register women sent out confusing registration information. New voters should verify their registrations with county clerks. Also during the primary, voters in one county reported that touch-screen DREs did not select their candidate. Voters should report such errors to poll workers should they recur.

EARLY VOTING

Any registered voter may vote early in person at a county clerk's office between Oct. 15 and Nov. 1, 2008.

WISCONSIN

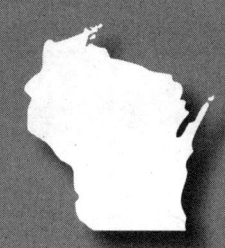

TO REGISTER TO VOTE, YOU MUST:

- Be a U.S. citizen
- Be a resident of Wisconsin for at least 10 days
- Be 18 years old
- Not have been convicted of treason, felony, or bribery (or, you must have had your civil rights restored)
- Not have been found by a court to be incapable of understanding the objective of the electoral process
- Not make or benefit from a bet or wage depending on the result of an election

Registration Deadline: Voters can register on Election Day at the polling place, in person at an election office by Monday, Nov. 3, 2008, or by mail by Wednesday, Oct. 15.

State Election Website:
http://elections.state.wi.us/faq_detail.asp?faqid=119&fid=27

http://elections.state.wi.us/category.asp?linkcatid=1773&linkid=270&locid=47

OFFICIALS TO CONTACT

Wisconsin's Government Accountability Board and municipal clerks oversee voting. The accountability board website has voter registration forms and instructions for the state's three options to register to vote: by mail up to three weeks before the election, in person up to the day before the election, and at the polling place on Election Day. Registration forms must be sent to the municipal clerks, whose contact information is listed on the accountability board website. Voters can also use an online tool to find their polling place.

VOTER ID REQUIREMENTS

People registering on Election Day must bring proof of residence to the polls. Photo and non-photo ID is accepted, including a valid Wisconsin driver's license or state ID card, an employee ID, tax bill for the current year, a rental lease, college ID, utility bill from within 90 days of the election, bank statement, paycheck, or government document with their name and address.

VOTING MACHINES

With the exception of Pierce County, Wisconsin used a mix of paper ballot voting systems and direct-recording electronic (DRE) systems with a voter-verified paper trail. Pierce County uses DREs with no paper trail. Voters with disabilities use ballot-marking devices.

EARLY VOTING

Registered voters may vote early in person at their municipal clerk's office after absentee ballots are ready through the day before the election.

WYOMING

TO REGISTER TO VOTE, YOU MUST:

- Be a U.S. citizen
- Be a resident of Wyoming
- Be 18 years of age on the day of the next election
- Not be convicted of a felony (or, you must have had your rights restored by a competent authority)
- Not be currently adjudicated as mentally incompetent

Registration Deadline: You can register at your polling place on Election Day.

State Election Website:
http://soswy.state.wy.us/election/vote.htm

OFFICIALS TO CONTACT

The secretary of state, county clerks, and town clerks oversee elections. There are three ways to register to vote in the state: by mail before the election, in person at the county or town clerk's office, and at the polls on Election Day. The state does not offer voter registration at its driver's license division. The secretary of state website has registration forms and a list of county clerks who can tell voters their polling place location.

VOTER ID REQUIREMENTS

ID is required, but the state accepts photo and non-photo ID. The preferred ID is a state driver's license, followed by a government-issue ID, school ID, or military ID. Voters can also use a current utility bill, bank statement, paycheck, or government document with their name and address.

VOTING MACHINES

Most of the state uses paper ballot voting systems, with three counties using a mix of paper ballot systems and direct-recording electronic (DRE) systems with a voter-verified paper trail. Voters with disabilities use ballot-marking devices.

EARLY VOTING

Wyoming has no early in-person voting, but any registered voter may vote early by mail. Contact a county clerk for an absentee ballot, which must be returned by Election Day.

NATIONWIDE VOTING RESOURCE LIST

VOTER REGISTRATION

PROJECT VOTE
www.projectvote.org
Project Vote has helped more than 4 million Americans in low-income and minority neighborhoods register to vote. It continues to work hard engaging low-income, minority, and other disenfranchised communities in the civic process.

ASSOCIATION OF COMMUNITY GROUPS FOR REFORM NOW (ACORN)
www.acorn.org
For the 2008 election, ACORN intends to help 1.2 million people register to vote in 26 states across the country in what will be the largest, nonpartisan voter registration effort in U.S. history.

OVERSEAS VOTE FOUNDATION
www.overseasvotefoundation.org
OVF is dedicated to doing one thing well: helping overseas American citizens and uniformed services voters register more easily and accurately than ever before. The website features a helpful directory of election officials.

LEAGUE OF WOMEN VOTERS
www.lwv.org
Dedicated to making democracy work for all citizens, the League has state chapters that work on issues from voter registration to proposals for political and electoral reform.

NONPROFIT VOTER ENGAGEMENT NETWORK
www.nonprofitvote.org
NVEN works to expand the role of America's nonprofits in voting and elections. Its website has a map with detailed voter registration and other election-related information for each state.

STUDENT PUBLIC INTEREST RESEARCH GROUPS
www.studentpirgs.org
Pioneers in youth voter registration and mobilization efforts, the Student PIRGs' New Voters Project is a nonpartisan effort to register young people and get them to the polls on Election Day.

DECLARE YOURSELF
www.declareyourself.com
Using the power of the media, celebrities, sports, and mobile and Internet technology, Declare Yourself blankets the landscape of popular culture, universities, and high schools with a simple, clear message: REGISTER and VOTE!

HEADCOUNT
www.headcount.org
Tapping into the live music scene, HeadCount reaches out to music fans with opportunities to register to vote and become socially active.

POLL WORKER RECRUITMENT

VOLUNTEER FOR CHANGE
www.volunteerforchange.org
Volunteer For Change was created by CREDO Mobile to make volunteering easier for busy people. In 2004, CREDO helped recruit over 15,000 Election Protection volunteers to be Election Day poll watchers.

NATIONWIDE VOTING RESOURCE LIST

LEGAL RIGHTS OF VOTERS

1-866-MYVOTE1
www.homepage.mac.com/cookhb/InfoVoter.net/infovotercontact.html

InfoVoter Technologies' Voter Alert hotline provides polling location information, registers and audio-archives voter complaints, and connects voters with election administration officials.

1-866-OUR-VOTE
www.nationalcampaignforfairelections.org/pages/election_protection

National Campaign for Fair Elections—the nation's largest nonpartisan voter protection coalition—sponsors this voter services hotline, staffed by lawyers who help callers overcome obstacles at the ballot box.

LAWYERS' COMMITTEE FOR CIVIL RIGHTS UNDER LAW
www.lawyerscomm.org

Formed in 1963 at the request of President John F. Kennedy, this nonpartisan, nonprofit organization uses the skills and resources of the private bar to address racial discrimination, including voting rights.

PEOPLE FOR THE AMERICAN WAY
www.pfaw.org

An aggressive advocate for the values that sustain a diverse democratic society, PFAW trains polling place monitors and advocates for voters in legal and policy settings.

AMERICAN CIVIL LIBERTIES UNION
www.aclu.org

The ACLU Voting Rights Project works to protect the gains in political participation won by minorities since passage of the Voting Rights Act in 1965. Some state chapters also represent ex-felons seeking to regain voting rights.

ADVANCEMENT PROJECT
www.advancementproject.org

Founded by a team of veteran civil rights lawyers, this legal action group works to dismantle institutional racism and secure the rights of minority voters.

BRENNAN CENTER FOR JUSTICE
www.brennancenter.org

Voting rights is a core mission of this nonpartisan public policy and law institute, which focuses on fundamental issues of democracy and justice.

MEXICAN-AMERICAN LEGAL DEFENSE AND EDUCATION FUND
www.maldef.org

MALDEF works to protect the civil and voting rights of the 45 million Latinos living in the U.S. and to empower the Latino community to fully participate in society.

NAACP (National Association for the Advancement of Colored People)
www.naacp.org

From the ballot box to the classroom, this organization champions social justice and voting rights, and has fought long and hard to ensure the voices of African Americans would be heard.

NATIONWIDE VOTING RESOURCE LIST

SENTENCING PROJECT
www.sentencingproject.org
By engaging in policy reform, litigation, public education, and voter registration, the Right to Vote Campaign aims to remove barriers to voting by people with felony convictions.

COMMON CAUSE
www.commoncause.org
Common Cause is committed to ensuring voting rights for all Americans, safeguarding voting systems and holding election officials accountable to the public interest.

CAMPAIGN LEGAL CENTER
www.campaignlegalcenter.org
This nonpartisan, nonprofit center works in the areas of campaign finance and elections, voting rights, political communication, and government ethics.

VOTER ACTION
www.voteraction.org
This national nonprofit organization seeks to ensure election integrity in the United States through legal advocacy, research, and public education.

DEMOS
www.demos.org
Demos works to reduce barriers to voter participation, support pro-voter litigation, encourage civic engagement, and advance a broad agenda for election reform.

ELECTIONLINE.ORG
www.electionline.org
This nonadvocacy website provides up-to-the-minute news and analysis on election reform, including a digest of election-related press clips.

STUDENT ASSOCIATION FOR VOTER EMPOWERMENT
www.savevoting.org
Founded and run by students, this nonpartisan group's mission is to increase youth voter turnout by removing access barriers and promoting stronger civic education.

VOTING MACHINES AND ELECTRONIC VOTING

VOTERSUNITE!
www.votersunite.org
This nonpartisan organization focuses on educating election officials, the media, and the public, as well as providing activists with the information they need to work toward transparent elections in their communities. Its national digest of news reports has an emphasis on electronic voting.

VERIFIED VOTING FOUNDATION
www.verifiedvoting.org
The organization champions reliable elections and supports a requirement for voter-verified paper ballots on electronic voting machines. An online map (verifiedvoting.org/verifier) identifies the election equipment used in each state.

ELECTION DEFENSE ALLIANCE
www.electiondefensealliance.org
EDA brings together citizen activists across the nation in a coordinated campaign for transparency and integrity in local, county, state, and national elections.

Notes

1. InfoVoter Technologies. "866.MYVOTE1: Primary Season 2008, Lessons Learned." Submitted to the House Committee on Administration, April 9, 2008 hearing.
2. Center for the Study of the American Electorate. "Turnout Exceeds Optimistic Predictions: More Than 122 Million Vote, Highest Turnout in 38 Years." Press release and accompanying study, January 14, 2005.
3. Mark, David. "States Brace For Record Turnout." *The Politico*, March 24, 2008.
4. Moore, Martha T. "States See Leap in Voter Registration." *USA Today*, April 6, 2008. http://www.usatoday.com/news/politics/election2008/2008-04-06-voterregistrations_N.htm?csp=34
5. Wolf, Richard. "Legal Voters Thrown Off Rolls." *USA Today*, January 2, 2008. http://www.usatoday.com/printedition/news/20080102/1a_lede02.art.htm
6. Hastings, Deborah. "Is Your Name on the Voting List?" Associated Press, March 2, 2008.
7. Rosenfeld, Steven. Author interview.
8. Stewart, Nikita. "10,000 Special Ballots Being Counted: A Crush of Voters and Unanticipated Turnout Caused a Shortage of Paper," *Washington Post*, February 16, 2008. B02.
9. Miller, Stacie. "The Real Story of the Pennsylvania Primary." Lawyers Committee for Civil Rights Under Law e-mail, April 25, 2008. http://www.nationalcampaignforfairelections.org/page/m/6fbe425e4c6b3145/GSgs0t/VEsh/
10. Hall, Bob. "Answer Related To Granville Co Problems At Polls." BlueNC.com, May 6, 2008, e-mail listserve. http://bluenc.com/the-fix-is-in-already%21%21
11. Associated Press. "Florida Can Bar Voters Who Have Problematic IDs." *Miami Herald*, April 4, 2008.
12. Weaver, Jay. "Judge: Deadline To Fix Voter Registrations Fair." *Miami Herald*, March 25, 2008.
13. Working Paper, Washington Institute for the Study of Ethnicity and Race, "The Disproportionate Impact of Indiana Voter ID Requirements on the Electorate," November 8, 2007. http://depts.washington.edu/uwiser/documents/Indiana_voter.pdf
14. Urbina, Ian. "Voter ID Battle Shifts to Proof of Citizenship." *The New York Times*, May 12, 2008.
15. Rosenfeld, Steven. "The Most Important Election Case Since Bush v. Gore?" AlterNet.org, November 20, 2007. http://www.alternet.org/rights/68368/
16. Rosenfeld, Steven. "Election Day 2007: New ID Laws Disenfranchise Voters." AlterNet.org, November 7, 2007. http://www.alternet.org/rights/67161
17. Lawyers Committee for Civil Rights Under Law. "Election Protection Fields Nearly 800 Calls During North Carolina and Indiana Primary Elections." PRNewswire, May 6, 2008. http://interestalert.com/story/05060000aaa05a3d.prn/siteid/DEMOCRAT/democrats.html
18. Rosenfeld, Steven, Author interview.
19. InfoVoter Technologies, recorded calls to 1-866-MYVOTE1 hotline, during May 6, 2008 Indiana Primary. www.myvote1.com
20. National Conference of State Legislatures, "Requirements for Voter Identification." http://www.ncsl.org/programs/legismgt/elect/taskfc/voteridreq.htm
21. Jadhav, Adam. "Voter Citizenship Bill Could Ignite Old Fight." *St. Louis Post-Dispatch*, April 20, 2008.
22. Urbina, Ian. "Decision Is Likely to Spur Voter ID Laws in More States." *The New York Times*, April 29, 2008.
23. Ibid. Same as 14.
24. Lida Rodriguez-Tasseff and Alexandra Wayland. "Disaster Looms Again On Election Day in Florida." *Miami Herald*, March 31, 2008. http://www.miamiherald.com/851/v-print/story/476926.html
25. Bill Turque. "To Avoid Jams, More Voting Machines Sought." *Washington Post*, February 19, 2008. B05.
26. Daniel Scarpinato and Josh Brodesky. "Election Problems Linked to Turnout." *Arizona Daily Star*, February 7, 2008. http://www.azstarnet.com/sn/print/DS224009
27. Rosenfeld, Steven. Author interview, March 2008.
28. Ibid. Same as 10.

Notes

29. Wolf, Richard. "High Voter Turn Out Prompts Resource Concern for Nov." *USA Today*, February 28, 2008. http://www.usatoday.com/news/politics/election2008/2008-02-28-Turnout_N.htm
30. Goff, Lisa. "Quick Study: Voting Machines." *Reader's Digest*, June 2008 edition. http://readersdigest.us/your-america-inspiring-people-and-stories/quick-study-voting-machines/article58348.html
31. Rosenfeld, Steven. Author e-mail, April 2008.
32. Editorial, "Managers Developing Anxiety about Nation's 2008 Elections." The Norman Transcript. http://www.normantranscript.com/opinion/local_story_338002419/resources_printstory
33. Editorial. "Casting Ideas For Better Count of Votes Next Time." *The Mercury News*, February 18, 2008.
34. Bellandi, Deanna. "History of Corruption Clouds Primary In Northern Indiana." Associated Press, May 7, 2008.
35. Davey, Monica. "Technical Factors Cited in Slow Results." *The New York Times*, May 8, 2008.
36. Associated Press. "Provisional Ballots, Missing Names on Voter Lists Cause Election Holdups." *Reno Gazette-Journal*, March 3, 2008. http://news.rgj.com/apps/pbcs.dll/article?AID=/20080303/NEWS19/803030327/1321/NEWS&template=printart
37. Rosenfeld, Steve, Author interviews.
38. Ibid. Same as 6.
39. Toohey, Marty. "Hundreds of Area Voters Might Have Registrations Cancelled: County, State Officials Blame One Another." *Austin-American Statesman*, January 17, 2008.
40. Ryman, Anne and McKinnon, Shaun. "Super Confusion at Arizona Polls." *The Arizona Republic*, Feb. 5, 2008
41. Clark, Heather. "AP Centerpiece: Voters, Poll Workers Question Accuracy of Lists." *Las Cruces Sun-News*, February 25, 2008.
42. Rosenfeld, Steven. "Super Tuesday's Voting Glitches." AlterNet.org, February 6, 2008. http://www.alternet.org/democracy/76233/
43. Rosenfeld, Steven. "Bad Voter Lists May Have Botched New Mexico's Democratic Caucus." AlterNet.org, February 8, 2008. http://www.alternet.org/democracy/76399/
44. Ibid. Same as 42.
45. Stewart, Nikita. "D.C. Council Member Scolds Elections Chief for Primary Voting Problems." *Washington Post*, February 15, 2008.
46. Buford, Talia. "Some Voters Hit Snags." *The Providence Journal*, March 5, 2008.
47. Rosenfeld, Steven. Author interview.
48. Palast, Greg. "The Great Florida Ex-Con Game." *Harper's Magazine*, 3/2/02.
49. Robert Fitrakis, Steven Rosenfeld and Harvey Wasserman. What Happened in Ohio? A Documentary Record of Theft and Fraud in the 2004 Election. (New York, The New Press, 2006). 13.
50. Weber, Lucy. "Purged Voting Rolls to be Fixed: Names of 10,000-plus Madison County Voters Expected to be Restored in Time for Tuesday Primaries After Snafu." *Clarion Ledger*, March 6, 2008.
51. Rosenfeld, Steven. "Voter Purging. A Legal Way for Republicans to Swing Elections?" AlterNet.org, September 11, 2007. http://www.alternet.org/rights/62133/
52. Ibid. see 51.
53. King, Brad. Co-director Indiana Election Division. e-mail, May 6, 2008.
54. Editorial. "Shirking A Voting Law: Requirement to Help Low-Income People Register is Being Neglected." *Las Vegas Sun*, March 2, 2008.
55. Associated Press. "Some Counties to Open Additional Early Voting Sites." *Winston-Salem Journal*, February 23, 2008.

Notes

56. Rosenfeld, Steven. "Department of Veterans Affairs Changes Policy On Helping Wounded Soldiers Register To Vote." AlterNet.org, May 1, 2008. http://www.alternet.org/democracy/84050/
57. Rosenfeld, Steven. "VA Retreats on Voter Registration Efforts for Wounded Veterans." AlterNet.org, May 8, 2008. http://www.alternet.org/democracy/84871/
58. Manning, Carl. "Proof of Citizenship Before Registration is Debated in Kansas." *Kansas City Star*, February 17, 2008.
59. Brennan Center For Justice at NYU School of Law. "Citizens Without Proof: A Survey of Americans' Possession of Documentary Proof of Citizenship and Photo Identification." Voting Rights and Election Series, November 2006.
60. Ibid. Same as 59.
61. Fields, Gary. "Felons' Voting Requests Pile Up." *The Wall Street Journal*, March 31, 2008.
62. SAVE's Blog, "It Can Be Easier to Register to Vote." July 16, 2007. http://www.savevoting.blogspot.com/
63. Ibid. Same as 62.
64. Kolasky, Ellen and Wondolowski, Lora. "Not Home, Not Welcome: Barriers to Student Voters." Project Democracy, League of Conservation Voters Education Fund, September 2004. P. 4.
65. Kiel, Lauren. "State Restrictions Inhibit Voter Registration." *The Harvard Crimson*, December 6, 2007. http://www.thecrimson.com/article.aspx?ref=521163
66. Ibid. Same as 65.
67. Ibid. Same as 15.
68. Schneider, Dorothy. "Purdue Students IDs Don't Pass Early Voting Test." *Lafayette Journal and Courier*, April 17, 2008.
69. Hastings, Deborah. "Photo ID Rule Causes Problems in Indiana." Associated Press, May 6, 2008.
70. Fitrakis, Bob. 2008 "As Ohio Goes…" In *Loser Take All: Election Fraud and the Subversion of Democracy, 2000-2008*. IG Publishing, Brooklyn, New York. P. 193.
71. Eriksen, Helen. "Thousands March in Prairie View For Voting Rights." *The Houston Chronicle*, Feb. 20 2008.
72. Doster, Adam. "One Student, No Vote: Activists Across The County are Organizing Students to get a Fair Shake at the Polls." *The American Prospect*, December 6, 2007. http://www.prospect.org/cs/articles?article=one_student_no_vote
73. Stewart, Warren. Author interview.
74. Ibid. Same as 72.
75. DeclareYourself.org. "Registration Info/FAQ." http://www.declareyourself.com/voting_faq/voting_faq.html
76. Ibid. Same as 65. P. 9.
77. Dutton, Audrey. "Voter Registration Rejections Sent To 17-year-old Voters." Gazette.net, May 7, 2008. http://www.gazette.net/stories/050708/chevnew203721_32416.shtml
78. Weir, Stephen. Author interview, August 2007.
79. Korber, Dorothy. "1 Million Votes Still Untallied in California." *Sacramento Bee*, February 14, 2008.
80. Tokaji, Dan. "The Problems with All-Mail Elections." Election Law @ Moritz blog, March 13, 2008. http://moritzlaw.osu.edu/electionlaw/comments/articles.php?ID=125
81. Ibid. Same as 80.
82. Rosenfeld, Steven. "Vote by Mail, Go to Jail." *The Texas Observer*, April 18, 2008. Features. http://www.texasobserver.org/article.php?aid=2738
83. Wang, Tova Andrea. "Bringing Voting Rights To Overseas and Military Voters." The Century Foundation Issue Brief, 2007. http://www.tcf.org
84. Rafferty, Scott. Author interview, April 2008.
85. Hanson, Shelley. "W. Va. Soldiers Can Vote by Fax; E-mail May Be Added." *The Intelligencer. Wheeling News Register*, May 9, 2008.
86. Ibid. Same as 80.

Notes

87. Cressman, Derek. "Getting It Straight for 2008: What We Know About Vote By Mail Elections and How To Conduct Them Well." Common Cause Education Fund, 2008. http://www.commoncause.org/site/pp.asp?c=dkLNK1MQIwG&b=3790039
88. Ibid. Same as 87.
89. 2008-09 Voting Assistance Guide, Federal Voting Assistance Program, U.S. Department of Defense. http://www.fvap.gov/pubs/vag.html
90. California Voter Foundation. "Voting FAQ." http://www.calvoter.org/voter/faq.html#q1
91. Ibid. Same as 87.
92. Clarkin, Mary. "Willing To Serve, Not Able To Vote." *The Hutchinson News*, April 23, 2008.
93. Baldor, Lolita C. "Few States Allow Overseas Troops to Vote by E-Mail." Associated Press, April 27, 2008.
94. Ibid. Same as 50. Page 192.
95. Rather, Dan. "The Trouble With Touch Screens." HDNet, August 2007. http://www.hd.net/drr227.html
96. Zetter, Kim. "GAO Report Says Machines Likely Not Responsible for Florida CD-13 Election Mishap." Wired.com, February 27, 2008. http://blog.wired.com/27bstroke6/2008/02/gao-report-on-c.html
97. Ibid. Same as 49. Pages 192-193.
98. Ibid. Same as 49. Pages 192-193.
99. Harry Cook. Author interview, April 2008.
100. Zetter, Kim. "Phantom Obama Vote Appears on NJ Voting Machine." Wired.com, April 30, 2008. http://blog.wired.com/27bstroke6/2008/04/phantom-obama-v.html
101. Levine, Art. "Democratic Congress To Voters: What Election Problem?" AlterNet.org, May 5, 2008. http://www.alternet.org/democracy/84492/
102. Gross, Grant. "Study: Voters Prefer E-Voting, But Tech Has Limits." PCWorld.com, March 22, 2008. http://www.pcworld.com/article/id,143755-c,currentevents/article.html
103. Rosenfeld, Steven. Author interview.
104. Ingold, John. "Vote Scanners Still Face Doubts." *The Denver Post*, February 17, 2008.
105. Sims, Scarlet. "Chairman Blames Delay In Election Results on Bad Luck." *The Morning News*, February 6, 2008.
106. Rosenfeld, Steven. Author interviews, March 2008.
107. League of Women Voters. "Guest Column: Poll Workers Important To The Election Process." *The Paper of Montgomery County*, April 24, 2008. www.thepaper24-7.com
108. InfoVoter Technologies, recorded calls to 1-866-MYVOTE1 hotline, during May 6, 2008 Indiana Primary. www.myvote1.com
109. InfoVoter Technologies, recorded calls to 1-866-MYVOTE1 hotline, during May 6, 2008 North Carolina Primary. www.myvote1.com
110. Metinko, Chris. "Heavy Turnout Cited For Ballot Shortage." *Contra-Costa Times*, February 7, 2008.
111. Spivack, Miranda S., "Voters Persevere Despite Shortages, Lines." *The Washington Post*, February 13, 2008.
112. Nietfeld, Ashley. "Legislation Brings Potential For Satellite Voting in Ford County." *Dodge Globe*, February 29, 2008.
113. Peryam, Jennifer. "Rokita Supports Vote Center Legislation." *Times-Union*, March 14, 2008.
114. Breakey, Patricia. "Board Considers Poll Site Removals." *The Daily Star*, March 28, 2008.
115. Meyers, Donald W. "Utah County Demotes Elections Boss After Voting Troubles." *Salt Lake Tribune*, March 7, 2008.
116. Ibid. Same as 49, p. 189.
117. Ibid. Same as 49, p. 79-81.
118. Nash, James. "Audit of Primary Votes Asked: Brunner Wants 11 Ohio Counties to Volunteer." *Cincinnati Enquirer*, March 25, 2008.

Author Acknowledgments

I would like to thank Beth Sauerhaft and Danya Sauerhaft for their love and support during this project. Special thanks also go to my parents, whose support has been unwavering through all my journalistic endeavors.

This project would not have been possible without contributions from many people. AlterNet's staff deserves praise, but especially Don Hazen, Liz Mullaney, Elijah Nella, Shelana deSilva, and Jan Frel. Many people reviewed the manuscript and made helpful suggestions, including Warren Stewart, Tova Wang, Susan Dzieduszycka-Suinat, Marina Meci, Bob Fitrakis, Elizabeth Westfall, Sujatha Jahagirdar, Charles Jackson, Miles Gerety, Heather Jones, Sally Engelfried, and Tai Moses. Others to be thanked for their support of my reporting include Michael Slater, Mark Crispin Miller, Gerry Hebert, David Becker, Wendy Weiser, John Bonifaz, Bill Stetson, Jane Stetson, Toni Whiteman, Harry Cook, Erin Ferns, Wendy Wendlandt, Diane Shamis, Tim Carpenter, John Gideon, Paul Sullivan, Scott Rafferty, Rick Hasen, Art Levine, Brad Friedman, Chanelle Hardy, and LaShawn Warren.

AlterNet Books Acknowledgments

Thank you to The Election Administration Fund of the Tides Foundation, the Bauman Family Foundation, and Working Assets for their generous support in helping us to publish and distribute this book.

About the Author

Steven Rosenfeld is a Senior Fellow at AlterNet.org, where he reports on elections from a voting rights perspective. Previously, he was Executive Producer of RadioNation with Laura Flanders, a progressive talk show heard on more than 100 Air America Radio and public radio stations.

He is co-author of *What Happened in Ohio: A Documentary Record of Theft and Fraud in the 2004 Election* (The New Press, 2006), and *Making History in Vermont: The Election of a Socialist to Congress* (Hollowbrook Publishing, 1992). An award-winning journalist, he has been a staff reporter at National Public Radio, Monitor Radio, TomPaine.com, and at daily and weekly newspapers in Vermont.

ALTERNET CITIZEN PUBLISHERS

AlterNet would like to extend a warm thank you to our Citizen Publishers. By contributing to the publication of this book, you are participating in a new citizen-powered media model. You are helping to support AlterNet's publishing effort, including making sure this book is in the hands of thousands of people working on campaigns, registering voters, and casting their ballots all over the country.

Help continue to spread the word about voter empowerment far and wide. Please visit www.AlterNet.org/CountMyVote to order additional copies of *Count My Vote*. Bulk discounts are available.

Welcome to the AlterNet publishing family.

Babatunde Abdullah
Tracy Abell
Allan Abrams
Lynn Abrams
Joan Abruzzo
Maxine Adams
Thomas Adams
Connie Adler
Daniel Aeschliman
Paul Ahern
MaryJane Akel
Phyllis Akif
Gerald Aksherian
Timothy Alexander
David Allan
Julie Alley
Louise Altman
Effie Ambler
Evan Anderson
Evie Anderson
Marv Anderson
Rosemary Anderson
Charles Andres
Stephanie Andrews
Margaret Andrietsch
Trudy Anschuetz
John Anshus
Dennis Antenore
Dorothy Anthony
Judit Apte
Janet Archer
Sigurd Arnesen
Reverand Dr. Jude Arnold
William Arnold
Meg Arteaga
Justina Ashley
Michael Atkins
John Atlee
Elizabeth G. Atterbury
Dale Axelrod
Mary Axford
Lauren Ayers
Ina Ayliffe
Ina Ayliffe
James Azzara
Barbara Babbitt
Marc Bachrach
Amy Baglan
Charles Bailey
Susan Baird
Vicki Baker
Lon Ball
Travis Ball
Cindy Ballou
Janet Barber
Allan Barclay
Nancy Bardos
Kathleen Barker

Harriet Barlow
Jacqueline Barnes
Peter Barnes
Erin Barnes
Roanne Barnett
Maiyim Baron
Brian Barrick
William Barrows
Paul Bartline
Herbert Bartling
Marcia Barton
Lonna and Alan Baum
Barbara Beach-Moody
Louisa Beal
D. Beardman
Brian R. Beckwith
David Beebe
R.W. Behan
Nancy Behling
Shayne Bell
Barbara Bellomy
Marcia Bennison
Phyllis Benstein
Thomas Berkley
David Berkshire
Deanna Berkson
Ahn Thackrey Berry
Joseph Bertz
Brandy Betz
Kay Beynart
Suzanne Biegel
Carrie Biggs-Adams
James Bishop
Ann Bixby
Lyle Black
William Blaesing
Teresa Blakely
John Bland
Linda Blasko
Kevin Bleich
Vicky Block
Coletta Bly
Judith Bodner
Duane Bogart
Kim Bogue
Chris Bohnert
James Bonaventure
Pat Boni
Elaine Booth
Lea Borden
Ann Bornstein
Ronald and Mary Bosch
Robert Bostick
Garry Bouffard
Ted Braun
Paula Breen
Lu Brenman
Ernest Brennaman

Kevin Briggs
Betty Brill
Charlotte Brody
Scott Brookes
China Brotsky
Christopher Brown
Matthew Brown
Melina Brown
Ricardo Brown
Sharon Brown
Marilyn Bruning
Bill Bruno
Phillip Bryant
Mary Budinger
Linda Budowski
David Buetow
Christian Burgess
James Burke
Charles Burkhardt
Kenneth Burres
Lonnie Burris
Yonca Bursali Ahmed
Diedre Bush
Melanie Bush
Bill Bushnell
John B. Butler
Michael Butler
Sam Butler
Colleen Butterfield
Mitzi Cagle, RN, BSN
Louise Calabro
Alex Caldwell
Wayne Caldwell
Jason Call
William E. Camp R
Stephanie Campbell
Thomas Campbell
William Carlin
Lori Carpenos
Jill Carpenter
Leonard Carrier
Ralph Carroll
Julie Carter
Mary Carter
Marshall Carter-Tripp
Dan Cash
Patt Castro
Ronald Cazares
Lisa Chadwick
Jane Chamberlain
Susan Chandler
Irene Chang
David Chaskes
Claudia Chaufan
John Chendo
Melissa Chesnut-Tangerman
Donna Childs
Jery Chilson

David Chipman
Donna Chow
John Chrisman
Ellen Chung
Edward Ciaccio
Judith Clancy
Colleen J. Clark
David Clark
David Clark
Donald Clark
Donald Clark
Frank Clark
Susan Clark
Steve Claus
Stan Claussen
David Clavelle
Barbara Clawson
Tory Clinesmith
Amanda Coalier
Ken Cobler
Jason Cockrell
Jill Cody
Michele Cohen
R. Cohn
Lester Cole
Barbara Collins
Judith Collison
James J. Cook
Cynthia Corbett
Ann Corley Silverman
Charlotte Costa
Yolande Cote
William Coughlan
Barbara Coulson
Sam Cowan
Steven Craddick
Sharon Crane
Jim Crawford
Charles E. and Susan S. Craze
Shirley Crenshaw
Carol Crooks
Sally Crosby
Nancy Crump
Drew Cucuzza
Diana Cunningham
Peter Cushnie
Nancy Cushwa
Katie Custer
Ron Cypert
George Daicos
Bonnie Dale-Bannister
Brett Dalton
Michael D'Amico
Wendy Darling
Kathleen Daugherty
Rikk David
Carolyn Davis

ALTERNET CITIZEN PUBLISHERS

Larry Davis
Margaret R. Davis
Peggy Cooper Davis
Ralph Davis
Roderick Davis
Thomas E. Davis
Nancy Davlantes
Jeanine Dawson
Terence Day
Laura Deal
Kenneth Deed
Anita P. DeFrantz
Shannen Delaney
Shirley DeMarco
Robert denBleyker
Georgetta H. Denhardt
Design By Strom
Marshall E. Deutsc
Velda Dey Curtis
P. Dominic DiBlasi
Paul Dietterich
Andrea DiLorenzo
Jeff Divers
Susie Diwald
Cynthia Dixon
Nancy J. Dobbins
Herman Dobbs
Patricia Donnell
Robert Dorst
June-Marie Dosdos
Stuart Dowty
Tim Aaron Doyle
Annette Drager
Peggy Drake
David Droge
Amanda DuBois
Susan Duerksen
Gloria Dumler
Jerry Duncanson
Josh Dunhamwood
Michael Duniho
Ginger Duran
Jean Durel
Nicholas Dykema
Jules Dykes
Cheryl Dykstra
Sandra Eagle
John Earl
Jane Earle
Inger Easton
Tim Ebrahimy
Nancy Edison
Scott Edwards
Kaci Elder
Sally Elesby
Rose Mary Elizondo
Andrea Sherrel Ellis
Donna Ellis
Janet Ellis
Durr Elmore
Lauran Emerson
John S. English
Howard Ennes
Richard Erskine
Raphael Esch
Martha K. Eskridge
Douglas Estes
Robert Evans
Maxine Ewig
Michael Fagans
James Faris
Lori Faulkner
Chuck Femec
Betsy Fenhagen
Teresa Fetter
Ed Finkelstein

Susan A. Fischer
Julius Fisher
Mark Fisher
John J. Fitzgerald
Naheed Flake
Richard Flanagan
Martha Fleischman
Donna Fleming
Joanne Fleming
Phyllis Fletcher
Elmerine Ann S. Flint
Rodney Florence
Elizabeth Flores
Gene W. Floyd
John Foley
Mickey Foley
Liana Forest
Caswell Forrest
Deborah Fort
Nettie Fowler
Jacquelyn Franklin
Gerald Frattini
Jack Frenkel
Terry Frewin
Milena Frieden
Karen Friedman
Meredyth Friend
Scientz from Canada
Jean Froneberger
Peg Futrell
Nivair Gabriel
Elizabeth Galbreath
Richard Gale
Heather Gamberg
Paige Garberding
Marco Garcia
Brian Garfield
Stan Geddes
Jon Christopher Geissmann
Judith Gengler
Douglas Gerleman
David Gerratt
Robert Getsla
Jon Gettel
Mindy Gewuerz
Marven Gibson
David Gilbert
John Gilbert
Margie Gilbert
Jacquelyn Giles
Peter Gillespie
Joni Gilton
Robert Ginsberg
Barbara Ginsburg
Robert Paul Glassen
Gordon Glick
Jeffrey Goddard
Barry Goldbarg
Daniel Goldberg
R. David Goldberg
Gail Golden
Janet Goldner
L. Lynnie B. Golon
Julie Gomoll
Edmund Good
Robert Goodrich
Henry Gordon
Sarah Gorin
David Graber
Patricia Gracian
Robert Gramenz
Brenda Grant
Marianne Grant
Stephen Gray
Anthony Greco
Ken Greenberg

Jack Greenhut
Lloyd Greenwell
Becky B. Gregory
Gary Greif
Eddie Griffiths
David Griscom
Thomas Grismer
Jane H. Gruen
Christopher Grundy
Ron Gutek
M. Faye Hadley
Lawrence C. Hager
Krista Haimovitch
Shabu Haji
Robert Hakes
Dan Hale
Gina Hale
Luanna Hale
Cecile Hall
James Hall
Terry Hall
Tim Hallen
Jeffrey Hallett
Lawrence Halperin
Joan Hamel
Bonni Hamilton
Gail Hamilton
Keith Handy
Ron Hankins
David Hannah
Robert M. Hanselman
Pauline Harding
Rick Harlan
Gail Harper
Gary Wood Harper
Roger H. Harrell
James Harrington
Don Harris
Jeannette Harris
Paul Harris
Brenda Harrison
Culver Harrison
Evelyn Harrison
Linus Hart
Bartlett Harvey
John Harvey
Alan Harwood
Robert Hatch
Joyce Hawes
Patricia Hawk
Joel Hawthorne
Sabrina Hayden
Dave Haynie
Sharon Hays
Rosalyn Hedman
Patricia Hefner
Bryna Hellman
Nathan Henderson-James
Emily Herbert
Rocio Hernandez
Dona Hertel
Michael Hetz
Brian Hiatt
John Hicks
L.D. Hieber, Jr.
Andy Hilgartner
Catherine Hill
Nancy Hilliard
June S. and Philmour B. Hillman
F. Earline Hittel
Florence Hochman
Trudi Hoekstra-Kubik
Don Hoffman
David Hofstatter
Kathleen Hogan

K.M. Hogarth
Delphine Hogston
Jack Hoke
John Holland
Ardent Hollingsworth
Marilyn Holmes
Harold Holoun
Timothy Holtz
Elizabeth Hoobler
S. W. Hood
Patricia Hooper
Aaron Horine
William Hory
Jerold Hubbard
Douglas Hunt
James W. Hunt
Allan Hunt-Badiner
Oregon Hunter
Robert Huotari
John Hutchcroft
Charlotte Hutchison
Lynn Hyndman
Sarah Ingersoll
Jonathan Inskeep
Thomas Ivester
Magnolia Izquierdo
Carolyn Jackson
Karen Jackson
Kathleen Jackson
Robert Jackson
Janet Jai
Fredi Jarmel
Kimberly Jarrett
Bruce Jenkins
Archie Jennings
Rhonda Jessee
Bruce Jewell
Angel Jimenez
Elizabeth Johns
Dean Johnson
Georgeann Johnson
Kevin Johnson
Mary K. Johnson
Randall Johnson
Veronica Johnson
Ann Jones
Linda F. Jones
Michael Jost
Marti Joyce
William Junor
Lois Kain
Amy Kallal
Diane Kamp
Peggy Kamuf
Herman Kane
Marshall Kaplan
Gary Karchg
Terry Karjalainen
Bruce Katz
Raymond Katz
Jody Kay
Katy Kay
Edward Kazala
Ryan Kegley
Chris Kelly
H. Kelly
H. David Kelly
John Kelly
Dexter R. Kemp Jr.
Janice Kendall
Dr. Lawrence Kent
Evan Keraminas
Rita Kiley
William Kilgore
J.E. Kim
Joseph Kiss

ALTERNET CITIZEN PUBLISHERS

Steven Klarer
Clarice Klepadlo
Linda Kliewer
Richard Knaub
Kris Knight
Jeff Knoop
Ronald Kohn
Kyle Konetzke
Todd Koons
Carolyn Koper
William Kopf
Susan Koppelman
Karie Korporaal
Joshua Kroll
Gregory Kruse
Gary Kuhn
Hal Kurz
Cassandra L Kyle
John Kyper
La Razza Films
Debbie Lackowitz
Athena LaFlamme-Edwards
Vasudevan Lakshminarayanan
Ann Lamb
Robert J. Lane
James Lange
Nicki Langewis
Mary Langley
Denise Larocque
Mr. Kim E. Larsen
Beth Larson
David Lasagna
Robyn Lauster
Judith Lautner
Chuck Lawhead
Karen Lawson
Peter R. Lawson
Frank and Dee Lawton
Pamela Lazos
Tarika Lea
Geralyn Leannah
Debbi Lee
Kenneth Lee
Lynn Lee
Valerie Lee
Megan Lehmer
Bill Leon
Esther Leonelli
Anne Leslie
Rob Levy
John Lewis
Kenneth Lewis
Joan Lichterman
Errol Lima
Laurie Lindberg
Lorie Lindsey
Lois Lineal
Jiri Lipa
Pamela Lippe
Dr. Richard Lippin
Nancy E. Liss
Lawrence Litvak
Tony Litwinko
Todd Lockwood
William D. Lockwood
Lyn H. Lofland
Gerry Long
Robert Long
Sharon Long
Kelle Louaillier
Br. Theodore Loucks, CFA
Ben Love
Benjamin Love
Michael Luckenbach
Joseph Luttner

Monica Maass
Pamela Maccabee
Judith Maclean
Kate Madison
Ali S. Malaikah
Chris Malis
Frank Mallalieu
Andre Maloney
Linda Maloney
James and Kaija Maloon
Milton Mankoff
Andy Mannle
Ingrid Marcroft
Catherine Margerin
Esti Marpet
Carol Marsh
Martin Marshall
A.J. Martin
Pia Massie
Karen Mathews
Yuki Mathias
Deborah Mattingly Conner
Robert May
Jill Mayer
Diane Mayr
Lucia McBee
Michael McCabe
Steve McCann
Patsy McCook
Laurice McCoy
John McDevitt
Ray McGovern
Gerald McKee
Patrick Mckenna
Terrie Mckenna
Mary McMorris
Forest McNeir
Leesa McVay
Cathryn Mecham
Media in the Public Interest
Richard Meeker
Alan Meerow
David Mendoza
William Meredith
Karen J. Merry
Jamie Metzler
Jane Meyer
Sylvia M. Meyer
Ellen Meyers
Eneida Michelson
Donna Middlehurst
Danielle Miele
Rhoda D. Miether
Ruthe Milan
Holly Millar
Francine Miller
Jphn Miller
Karen Miller
Mary Lou Miller
Wendy Miller
Stuart A. Miner
Stefani Mistretta
Brian Mitchell
Jennifer Mittereder
Dave Moffatt
Louise Monaco
Evelyn Monahan
Mark Moniz
Kenneth Moore
David Morgan
Charlotte Morrison
Basho Mosko
Helen Mosley
James Mosteller
Marva Mouser
Lewis Moyse

Brigitte Mueller
Dimity Mueller
Steven Mull
Victoria Muniz
Frank Munley
Kathryn Munson
Edmond Murad
Dirk Murcray
Diana Murdoch
Lee Murdoch
Dick Murphy
Kelly Murphy
Verona Murray
Vasu Murti
Scott Muttersbaugh
Nancy Naples
Steve Nash
Noel Nehf
Mark Neiman
Claudia Nelson
Lorenzo Nencioli
David Nett
Robert Newhard
Annie Newman
Naomi Newman
William Nichols
Louis Nielsen
Mariana Nielsen
Jeff Noble
Gloria Norgang
Elizabeth Norris
John Norton
Debbie Nuss
Sharon Obeidallah
George O'Connor
Arliene Oey
John Officer
Deacon Allen Ohlstein
Reverend Gerald Oleson
Frederick Olson
Melissa Olson
CJ Ondek
Trish O'Neil
William O'Neil, Jr.
Leonard Oppenheimer
Sarah Ortman
Patricia O'Sullivan
Barbara Ottinger
Marca Ouida
Mieke Pagan
Susan Page
John Painter, Jr.
Hannah Pal-al
Francesca Palermo
Lynda Palevsky
Robert Pancner
Eva Pando Radford
Angela Papich
Richard Parr
Patricia Parraga
Brian Parrella
Stanley G. Parry
Puja D. Parsons
Heidi Patterson
Jean Pauline
Jill Paxton
Art Pearl
Constance Penley
Roberta Penn
Sharon Penprase
Elsin Perry
Robert Perry
Susan Perry
David Peters
Gerald J. Peterson
Gianna Phelps

Gay Phillips
Maxine Phillips
Michael Phillips
William Phillips
Tom Pickens
Jeri Pierson
Pinfolk
Diane Plantenga
Paul Platt
Cynthia Plockelman
Thomas Plum
Kim Pohl
Harry Pollitt
Lane Poncy
Debra Porta
Rachel Pratt
Nomi Prins
Beate Priolo
Robert Otis Pritchard
Engineous Productions
Billy Pruett
Alice Pulver
Mary Purves
Harriet Putterman
John Quigley
Philip Quinn
David Quist
Daniel Rafferty
Myra Ramos
Paul Ramshaw
Roberta Ransley-Matteau
Casey Reed
Jim Reed
Suzanna Reeder
Lawrence A. Reh
Fred M. Reinman
N.I. Renfrew
Alberto Restrepo
Lynn Rhea
Jim Rhyne
Lisa Rice
Philip Richardson
Joseph Richey
Jo Ann Richmond
Marlise Riffel
Laurie Rigelhaupt
Karen Riggs
Sharon Rippner
Suzanne Ristagno
Michael Rivas
Virginia Rivers
Richard Roast
Lisa C. Roberson
Laurie Robertson-Lorant
Nathan Robfogel
Terry Robinson
Tom Robischon
Dianne Rocheleau
Sarah Roche-Mahdi
Phil Rockey
Michael Rockliff
Ellen Roehl
Donald Roemer
David Rogers
Dawn Rogers
Robin Rogers Kostel
Catherine Roma
Pat Rose
Elana Rosen
Richard Rosen
Arthur Rosenfeld
Peter Joseph Rosenwald
Denise Ross
Carol Ross Stacy
Ruth Rugh
Nathan Rushton

ALTERNET CITIZEN PUBLISHERS

Sharon Ruxton
Alix Sabin
Margaret Sacco
Lynn Saddleton
Jo Salas
Frances Salisbury
Joan C. Sanders
Sharon Sanders
Susan Sanders
John P. Sanders, Jr.
Carol Sanford
Nona Sanford
Brooke Santos
Zalman Saperstein
Dudley and Elizabeth Sarfaty
Paul Sauers
Kathy Saunders
Ansley Sawyer
Eric Schechter
Eric Schell
Elise Schlaikjer
Allan Schneidmiller
Janice Scholl
Gary Schreiner
Brina-Rae Schuchman
Rosemary Schumann
Daniel Schwartz
Linda Schwarz
Doug Scott
Judson Scott
Sharon Seabrook
Heidi Seekins
Nikki W. Seeler
Kate and Charles Segerstrom
Linda Seligson
Cathryn Sells
David Shafer
Carolyn Shaffer
Susan L. D. Shamblin
Cindy Shapiro
Marlene Share
Robin Share
Devin Shaw
Jim Shaw
Mickey Shell
Larry Sherk
Danielle Shillcock
Alan Shorb
Frank Shulman
George Sibley
Florence Siegel
Larry Silvey
Henry Simmons
Jerry Simon
Martha Simon
Kyle Simplot
Jared Simpson
Linda Simpson
William Sims
Nadia Sindi
Yvonne Siu-Runyan
Betty Skaggs
Eve Slatner
Jeff Sluyter-Beltrao
Andrew Small
Deborah Smith
Gregory Smith
James Smith
Kenneth Smith
Lanette Smith
Richard Harding Smith
Katrin Smithback
Marvion Snider
Thomas Snyder
William Snyder
Ernest Solit
Arthur Solomon
Hadley Solomon
Sally Sommer
Mason Sommers
David Sonneborn
Gregg Sorensen
Diane Souza-Chatman
Joan Spencer
Joey Sprague
Mena and Dave Sprague
Rose Sprungl
Randall St. Jacques
Christina Stableford
Gregory Stafford
Jed Staley
Elizabeth Standen
Keith Stanger
Kris Stanton-Trail
Janie Starr
Marilyn Steber
Russell Steele
Terry Stella
Phyllis Stenerson
Craig Stern
Rosalie Stern
Arin Stevens
Debra Stevens
Kathy Stevens
Nancy Stevens
Rita and George Stevens
Robert Stevenson
Douglas Stewart
Jeffrey Stewart
John Stickler
Robert Stimpert
Lural Stingley
Mary Jo Stockwell
Bill Stout
Michael Stout
Mildred B. Stout
Jerri Strasser
Andrew Strassman
Jerry Straughan
Russ Streiner
David Strom
Barbara Stuart
Vern Stulken
Avn Sturm
Alan Sukoenig
Mary Sullivan
Gerald Sutliff
Mike Svejcar
Merlin Swartz
Timothy Sweeney
Nancy Syburg
Paul Szymanowski
Tamaara D. Tabb
Wilkie and Patricia Talbert
Tarpaulin Sky Press
Joan Taylor
Renate Taylor
Vickie Taylor
William Taylor
Edith Teague
Martha Teeter
Judith Telingator
Scott Teresi
Sheila Thacker
Judith Tharinger
Dale Thaw
Thomas Thirion
Alan Thomas
Joanne Thomas
Leeya Thompson
Wayne Thompson
Bill Thwaites
Mary Alice Tierney
Maurice Tierney
Linda Tillitt
Gene Tinelli
Melba Tolliver
Joanie Tompkins
Janice Toole
PJ Torokvei
Leo H. Torres
Catherine Trainor
Clare Tremper
Marjorie Trifon
John Trinkl
Ronald Trojcak
Julia Tucker
Warren Turner
Jon Tveite
Catherine Twohill
Kim Tyler
Patricia D. Tyler
Steven Tyler
CC Ulatowski
Brian Ulm
Thomas Ulrich
Lauren Unruh
Roger Vaagen
Tracy Van Slyke
Phebe Vance
Nancy VanDermark
Susan VanKuiken
Gay Vaughn
Randall Vehar
Linda Veiga
Gail Vernon
Barbara Vickrey
Bruce Vida
Dottie Villesvik
Juli Viscardi
Zizi Vlaun
Renee Vollen
Robert von Tobel
Peacemakers of Schoharie County Voting Integrity Project
Lindsay Vurek
Barbara Waali
James Wack
Will Wagoner
Mike Waitt
Karen S. Walker
Ronald Wallace
John Wallack
David Walls
Tom Walls
Laurie Walters
Monty Walters
Laura Warfield
Michelle Warne-Crandlemire
Martha Warner
Wayne Warner
Elizabeth J. Wearley
Kevin Webb Rogers
Linda Webb Varian
Judy Webber
Ron Weiner
Edmund Weisberg
Jennifer Weiss
Jan Wells
Glenn Welsh
Wendy Wendlandt
Briana Wentworth
Adam Werbach
Mary West
John Westwood
Lucille Whalen
Ladie Whitaker
April L. White
Jennifer Whiteley
Robert Van Norman Whitford
Dolores Whitman
Kim Whittemore
Randi Wickliff
Robert M. Wierzel
Jarvis Wilcox
Andrew Wiley
David Wilk
Paul Wilkins
Clarence Wilkinson
David L. Williams
Judd Williams
Octavia Williams
Patrick Williams
Robert L. Williams
Brenda Williams, aka "Black Coffee"
Perde Williams, Jr.
Barrett Wilson
Dean Wilson
Franci Wilson
Lana Wilson
Susan Wilson
Karen Winckler
Robert L. Winder
Julie Winokur
Amanda May Winter
Liza Q. Wirtz
John Wise
Beverley Wiskow
Patricia Wisne
Sarah Witter
Richard Wolfe
Marion Wolk
Ann Wong
Wendy M. Wood
Jennifer Woodcock
Medora Woods
Mike Woods
Murphy Woodson
William Worden
Lewis Wright
Elissa Wurf
James Yanda
Bethany Yarrow
Rosalie Yelen
Gertrude Young
Grant Youngblood
Patricia Yurrita
Syed Zaidi
Marian Zaouk
Gail Zappa
Natalie Zarchin
Ann Zegler
Angela Zehava
Gil Zicklin
Audrey Zimmer
Angela Zito
Mark Zivin
Steven Zucker

ABOUT ALTERNET.ORG

AlterNet.org is an award-winning news magazine and online community that creates original journalism and amplifies the best of dozens of other independent media sources. Its mission is to inspire citizen action and advocacy on the environment, human rights and civil liberties, social justice, media, and health care issues. AlterNet's editorial mix underscores a commitment to fairness, equity, and global stewardship, and to making connections across generational, ethnic, and issue lines. AlterNet has won two Webby Awards for best web magazine and several Independent Press Awards for online political coverage. AlterNet was also named one of National Public Radio's five "Winners on the Internet."

ABOUT ALTERNET BOOKS

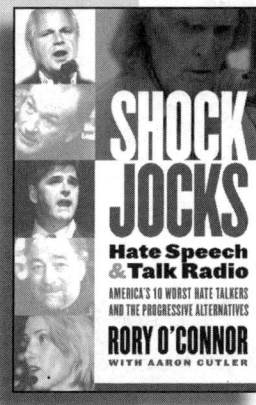

AlterNet Books was created to bring our readers a deeper and more insightful analysis of the progressive issues that matter.

Visit AlterNet.org/books today to order our other books!

Launched with *Young Dick Cheney: Great American*, AlterNet Books is a source of provocative thinking and high-quality writing.

Shock Jocks: Hate Speech and Talk Radio, our second book, highlights the politicized and often factually challenged world of talk radio and profiles the progressive alternatives fighting for airtime.

Count My Vote: A Citizen's Guide to Voting is our third book.

Water Consciousness is a comprehensive, solution-focused guide to the world's greatest environmental crisis. Edited by Tara Lohan, AlterNet's managing editor, *Water Consciousness* is designed to change the way people think about water. It assembles the leading environmentalists, including Bill McKibben, Vandana Shiva, Maude Barlow, Tony Clarke, Deborah Kaufman, Alan Snitow, and Wenonah Hauter, to delve into the crisis and what we can do about it. *Water Consciousness* also inspires. Authors cover conservation and efficiency, the role of new technology and design, and the need for policy that protects water for all people as a common trust and not a commodity. It is a book that will change not just your day-to-day activities but your thinking as well.

CREDO presents two ways to stand up for democracy in the 2008 election

TXT OUT THE VOTE

Sometimes all it takes is a little reminder. Make sure your friends and family vote this November 4 by sending a text message to their mobile phones. You write the message, and we'll send it for you on election day.

txtoutthevote.com

POLLWORKERS FOR DEMOCRACY

Protect the election and get paid! Sign up to be an official pollworker and make a difference on the front lines this fall.

credoaction.com/pollworkers

credoaction.com